Prayer Warrior:
The Making of a Great Intercessor

Nadine A. Anderson

To: Gabriel Oluwalayomi
Ruth cBoaz
Ruth 3:11

5/13/05

TRAFFORD

Printed in Victoria, Canada

A cataloguing record for this book that includes the U.S. Library of Congress Classification number, the Library of Congress Call number and the Dewey Decimal cataloguing code is available from the National Library of Canada. The complete cataloguing record can be obtained from the National Library's online database at: www.nlc-bnc.ca/amicus/index-e.html
ISBN: 1-4120-2778-0

TRAFFORD

This book was published *on-demand* in cooperation with Trafford Publishing. On-demand publishing is a unique process and service of making a book available for retail sale to the public taking advantage of on-demand manufacturing and Internet marketing. **On-demand publishing** includes promotions, retail sales, manufacturing, order fulfilment, accounting and collecting royalties on behalf of the author.

Suite 6E, 2333 Government St., Victoria, B.C. V8T 4P4, CANADA

Phone	250-383-6864	Toll-free	1-888-232-4444 (Canada & US)
Fax	250-383-6804	E-mail	sales@trafford.com
Web site	www.trafford.com	TRAFFORD PUBLISHING IS A DIVISION OF TRAFFORD HOLDINGS LTD.	
Trafford Catalogue #04-0606		www.trafford.com/robots/04-0606.html	

10   9   8   7   6   5   4   3

ACKNOWLEDGMENTS

I give honor, praise and glory to God for the inspiration of this book. To my beloved son Christopher McKenzie, in whom I am well pleased, I give praise for his patience and encouragements. Thank you for going through the fire with me, and coming out as pure gold. I also want to thank all my friends and family for allowing God to use them to produce an anointing in me. To my prayer partners I give you praise, without your prayers I could not have accomplished all that I needed to do in order to break barriers in my life. To my family, I pray that my walk before God will revolutionize your lives and give you a future with an expected end in glory. To my dearest brother, Pastor Billy and my darling sister, Princess Phina, thank you both for your encouragement's that sustained my faith and your walk before God that gave me hope and a future. Finally, to Pastor Dorothy Washington of Good News Church; I say thank you for answering the call of God on your life. I have learned the foundation for prayer, intercession and spiritual warfare under your leadership and effective teachings of the Word of God. Again, thank you.

INTRODUCTION

This book is about praying the word of God. It is simple and easy to read. It was born out of my desire to learn how to pray and get results. When I got saved, I did not know how to pray; however, I knew I could learn how to pray. As a child, I was taught the 23rd psalms. As a new christian, this was not enough for me, I wanted more. I did not know or comprehend the power of prayer but I wanted to walk upright before God and man and eliminate sin from my life. The day I gave my life to the Lord, I was expecting an instant miraculous transformation from a sinner to a mature christian. To my surprise this was not so and it disturbed me and made me very unhappy. I was tired of repenting weekly at the alter and crying like a child; I suddenly realized I could repent immediately when I sinned or was made aware of my sins, I also integrated daily repentance in my prayer life and time with God and I also repented of iniquities and things I was not aware of, such as secret sins. Psalms 51 made a major difference in my life. So, I pursued God with a passion to know him and his word. God drew me and revealed himself to me to the point I was able to speak to him from my heart with all honesty and sincerity. But he surprised me and spoke back to me in an audible voice which marveled me. I ask God to teach me how to pray and God told me where to find a book titled "HOW TO PRAY" I purchased the book for $5.00 and it changed my life. The booklet was written similar to this book and had 12 pages. When I had outgrown the booklet I gave it to a young lady and joined a prayer group at church and became a faithful intercessor. Many of the prayers in this book were conceived out of my own desires and struggles. While others were the divine inspiration of God; meaning, that God gave the scriptures and the titles to address issues I did not experience or desired. Please note that most of the scriptures in this book were taken form the King James Version of the bible, while other scriptures were taken from the New International Version, Living Bible and New Revised Standard Version of the bible. This book was the result of 5 years of hard work and much prayer and intercession. I pray that as you read this book and declare the word of God over your life, family, nation and situations that you will see God in his word and you will hear God speak to you clearly. I pray that you will find valuable treasures, hidden riches and wealth beyond measure in this book.

CONTENTS

PRAYERS   *PAGES*

Book I (The Prayer Warrior) 1
Salvation 7
Covenant of Salvation 10
Thanking God 11
Healing 12
Covering, Protection and Deliverance 13
Deliverance 17
Deliverance from the Wicked 18
Deliverance from Enemies 19
Deliverance from the Works of the Enemies 20
Deliverance from the Enemy's Defense 21
Deliverance of your Enemies into your Hands 21
Deliverance for God's People 22
Deliverance from Evil Men 24
Deliverance Power 25
Deliverance for God's Anointed 25
Deliverance of Possessions 27
Deliverance of the Righteous 27
Deliverance in the Dance 28
Deliverance from foes 29
Protection 31
Protection from Evil 32
Protection from Enemies 33
Protection from Fears 33
Protection from Evil Plans 34
Protection from the Blood 35
Protection Edging 36
Protection and Deliverance for Couples 36
Witchcraft and Enemies 39
To Forgive your Enemies 40
Envy and Jealousy 42
Warfare and Judgment 43

Warfare Stoned Walls 44

Warfare the Great Trees 45

Declaration to Satan 46

Practice no Evil 48

The Wrath of God 48

Possessing our Possession 49

President and Leaders 51

Wisdom to Lead 53

A New Beginning 54

The Lord's Guidance 55

Restoration 57

The Power of the Holy Spirit 59

The Anointing of God 60

God's Power to Man 62

Prayer for Ministry 63

Signs, Wonders, and Miracles 64

The Lord's Handmaiden 66

Fathers and Dads 67

Mothers and Moms 69

Child and Children 71

Deception and Error 73

What our Children Listen 73

What our Children Watch 73

Counsel for our Children 74

Blessings & Protection for Children & Friends 74

Children's Protection from Enemy 75

Journey and Traveling 75

Prodigal and Rebellious Children 76

God's Kingdom in your Child 76

My Daughter 77

My Son 79

Repenting Heart of a Son 80

Son's Future Wife 81

Daughter's Future Husband 81

Desires of the Heart for Family 82
Financial Prosperity 85
Prosperity 88
Prosperity of Couples 91
Desires of the Heart for Mates 92
Seeking a Husband 93
Confession of Faith 95
Book II (Praying the Psalms) 96
Page of Contents 97
Introduction 98
Book One 99
Book Two 105
Book Three 108
Book Four 110
Book Five 112
Book III (The Church Prayer Manual) 114
Contents 115
Introductions 116
History of Prayer & God's Response 119
Prayer for Pastor 122
Prayer for your Church 126
Book IV (Children's Prayer) 132
Contents 133
God's commandments 134
Our Father 134
My Obedience to God & Man 134
God is My Provider 135
Healing & Restoration 135
God's Commandments for My Life 136
God's Purpose for My Life 137
I am a Mighty Warrior for God 138
Prayer Ministry 140
Covering, Protection and Deliverance 141
To Forgive your Enemies 144

SALVATION

Have mercy upon me and my family God. Lord, blot out my transgressions for your name sake. Wash me from mine iniquity, and cleanse me from my sins. Purge me with hyssop, and I shall be clean, wash me, and I shall be whiter than snow. Hide thy face from my sins, and blot out all mine iniquities. Create in me a clean and pure heart O God and renew a right spirit of the Holy Ghost within me. Cast me not away form thy presence O Lord and take not thy Holy Spirit from me. Restore unto me the joy of thy salvation; and lift me up with your free spirit. I will teach sinners your ways and they shall be converted unto you and serve you as Lord, God and King, in Jesus name I pray. I declare my whole household is saved and walking upright before God. It is written as for me and my whole house we will serve the Lord. God, will save and deliver the seeds of the righteous; therefore, my seeds are saved for it is written the words that God has placed in my mouth shall not depart out of my mouth or my seeds mouth forever. Spirit of Babylon I command you in the name of Jesus to release my unsaved families, friends and enemies. God's of this world, in the name of Jesus I command you to loose the eyes and ears of the people. In the name of Jesus, I command the spiritually blind to see and the spiritually deaf to hear. Spirit of darkness I bind you in the name of Jesus and command the spirit of light to shine in the midst of you. Spirit of religion, I bind you in the name of Jesus and command you to loose your hold upon the chosen of the Lord. God's of this world, in the name of Jesus, I resist you and I command you to flee from

7

my unsaved families, friends and enemies. Satan, the blood of Jesus is against you and you have lost the battle for the souls of mankind in Jesus name. Spirit of pride, I bind you in the name of Jesus and cast you to the low place in the pit of hell and utter darkness. Evil and wicked spirits, I bind you in the name of Jesus and cast you out of the land into hell and utter darkness. Lying spirit and the spirit of error I bind you in the name of Jesus and command you to flee into hell and utter darkness. Spirits of Baal, I bind you in the name of Jesus and command you to go to hell and utter destruction. Spirit of python and spirit of serpent, I bind you in the name of Jesus and cast you into hell and outer darkness. Spirit of serpent, I crush your head in Jesus name. I cast you out of the land and command you to flee in Jesus name. Satan, the Lord rebukes you in Jesus name. Spirit of Lucifer the blood of Jesus is against you. Spirit of Satan and Lucifer I decree and render you powerless in Jesus name. I dethrone you of your high places in the name of Jesus and establish the throne of Jesus Christ in the places you have illegally dominated. Satan, I loose the sword of God against you in the name of Jesus. Satan, I loose the judgment and wrath of God against you in the name of Jesus. I break and dismantle all your weapons in the name of Jesus. I take back all the souls you have stolen in Jesus name. I take back all the grounds and territories you have stolen in Jesus name. Spirit of Satan and spirit of Lucifer, I discomfort you in the name of Jesus and command you to flee in Jesus name. I push back the forces of darkness in the name of Jesus and Satan's army to flee into outer darkness and distress. Spirit of whoredom, I bind your hands and your feet in the name of Jesus and I command you to flee to utter darkness. I loose the sword of God against you for utter destruction. I loose the arrows of God to shoot you down out of the heavens. I loose the angels of God to pursue you and the army of darkness to utter destruction. I loose the rod of correction to bring you into submission according to the word of God. I loose the spirit of truth upon the land in the name of Jesus. I loose the spirit of light upon the land in the name of Jesus I loose the angels of heaven to bring in the harvest of souls. I loose a revival upon the land in Jesus name. I loose the power of God upon the land in Jesus name. I loose the gifts of God upon the land in Jesus name. I loose the anointing of God upon the land in Jesus name. I loose the love, favor and mercy of God upon the land in Jesus name. I loose freedom and the spirit of liberty upon the land in Jesus name. I declare and loose deliverance upon the land in Jesus name. I bind Satan and his army in the name of Jesus and render them powerless to attack in any way shape or form, the army of God. In the name of Jesus, I loose the arrows of God into the enemies' camp. In the name of Jesus, I command the walls of the enemy's camp to crumble and fall to the ground. In the name of Jesus, I loose the army of God to pursue, overtake and utterly destroy the enemies of God. Jesus Christ is the rock of faith upon which I build the church. Jesus is the rock that the builder refused that has become the head corner stone. I loose the cities to be rebuilt upon the foundation of Jesus Christ. I plant the word of God in the land and command the tree of life to produce the fruits of the spirit in all the earth in Jesus name. I declare Zion is built upon Jesus, in Jesus name I pray. Amen.

COVENANT OF SALVATION

I am saved in the name of Jesus Christ. Therefore Christ shall be magnified in my body. I accept the call to live for Jesus Christ. I know that it will cost me everything to serve the Lord. I am more than willing to pay the price for His glory to be revealed in me. I make myself totally available for the use of God. God, will bring me before kings and queens. Nations will run unto me seeking the wisdom God, has placed within me. Men shall fear me because of the glory of the Lord that has risen upon me. Great shall be my peace for the greatness of God is seen in my daily walk with Jesus. Men shall see the fear of God written upon me. Men will see me and know that I am of God and no weapon that is formed against me shall prosper. I am a polished shaft in the hand of God and an arrow in his bow to shoot at his enemies at will. I am the Lord's battle-axe and a weapon of his warfare crafted for battles in heavenly places. I am like the warrior Joshua and the Prophetess Deborah, an instrument of war and a sharp threshing instrument. God, will cause me to lead a great and mighty army. Multitude of people will come to see how the Lord has established me. I am the voice of God. I speak with the voice of an oracle, for God has ordained me to be his mouthpiece. Many will reject me and many more will accept me but I have no fear for even so they rejected Jesus Christ, the only begotten son of the Most High God and the prophets that were before me. They that are of God will hear me but the world will not hear me. God will give me the power to cut down and destroy them that rise against me and would attempt to harm me in Jesus name.

THANKING GOD

Lord, I thank you for your mercy and your grace. I thank you for being my strong tower and my shield of defense. Lord, I thank you for giving me a new song and dance. I thank you for anointing me for the greater works. Lord, I thank you for giving the nations unto me and bringing the leaders of the nations unto me in Jesus name. Lord, I thank you for saving my entire family. I thank you for wealth, riches and prosperity. I thank you for making me a blessing to others. Lord, I thank you for making my name great upon the earth and causing the nations to fear me and honor me in Jesus name. Lord, I thank you for blessing me with favor and opening doors in my life that no man can close and closing doors in my life that no man can open. Lord, I thank you for making my way clear, established and rooted in the word of God. Lord, I thank you for the gifts of miracles, healing, prophecy, word of knowledge and discernment. Lord, thank you for my business, home, car, finance, children, sisters, brothers, mother and father. Lord, thank you for my aunts, uncles, cousins, nieces and nephews. Thank you for my friends, enemies and associates. In everything Lord, I give you thanks for it is your will for my life. Lord, I thank you for all the disappointments and the disasters in my life. For your word declares that everything works together for my good to bring me to an expected end. Lord, thank you for caring for me and providing for all my needs. You have fed me, clothed me and gave me shelter, for this Lord, I thank you and give you praise. Thank you for being my shepherd, for you have met all my needs and protected me from all evil.

Thank you for saving my soul from death and giving me eternal life. Thank you for making a way out of no way for me and thank you for blessing me when my enemies desired to curse me. Thank you for abounding me in blessings all the days of my life. Lord, I thank you for your love. Lord, thank you for being my friend and paying all my debts. God, I thank you for everything. God, I thank you for being so good to me in a world so vast and a vessel so fragile. Lord, I thank you that you are a savior, because I was poor, naked and wretched on my way to eternal death and damnation when you saved me. Lord, I thank you for the sacrifices of praise and my obedience to your will for my life in Jesus name. Lord, I thank you for your glory that is revealed in me. I am God's word made flesh for the glory of God. God, I thank you for ordaining and sanctifying me to walk into my true identity and destiny with you. Thank you God for causing me to walk into my pathway, that leads to life and godliness. I thank you Lord, for taking time to fellowship with me daily. I thank you for causing me to find you as I seek you with my whole heart. Amen.

HEALING

My father in heaven above, you have spoken and created life in me with your words. Therefore, I live and breathe in your words. I am full of life and vitality. No sickness, disease or infirmities invades or dwells in my holy body according to the word of God. I was healed before I became sick because you sent your word to heal me before the foundation of the world. The evidence of my healing is my faith and trust in God. The testimonies of the healed of the

Lord and my testimonies are the evidence of my faith. I command my body to function in perfect perfection according to the word of God. I command every organ, every tissue and every cell in my body to be healed, full of health and strength and operating in divine wholeness. I bind all sickness, all disease and all infirmities from operating in my body. I loose health, strength, wellness, wholeness and complete healing and restoration to my entire body, from the top of my head to the bottom of my feet, in the name of Jesus Christ. Lord, I thank you that you have sent your word and healed me. Jesus Christ is your word made flesh and was beaten with 39 stripes for my healing. God still heals. God is the same yesterday, today and forever, He never changes. God is still a healer and God is still in the healing business. God is bigger than sickness and diseases, whatever it is God is bigger. Lord, I thank you for granting me healing as a gift, a promise and a covenant. No longer will I accept sickness in my body, mind or spirit for with his stripes I was healed. By the beatings of Jesus Christ I was made whole in my body. I am totally restored from the curse of sin and death. I am saved by grace and covered under the blood of Jesus Christ the only begotten son of God. Come Holy Spirit breathe upon me the healing powers of your virtue and ignite an anointing in me to heal others in the name of Jesus Christ the anointed one of God sent to me in His glory. In the name of Jesus Christ, sickness, disease and infirmity I resist you and command you to flee for it is written if I resist the devil he will flee. I renounce and reject every curses sent against me in the spirit realm and in the natural for it is written cursed is the man that hangs upon a tree and Jesus

Christ bore all my curses upon the cross of Calvary; therefore, I declare my freedom from every curse. I render every curse sent against me and my family null and void and of no effect. For it is written that God has given me power over every work of the enemy and nothing shall hurt me because the Lord, God, Almighty has commanded his angels to protect and watch over me. No sickness and disease shall come near me or my dwelling for the Lord has built a wall of protection around me and has hedge me in the blood of Jesus Christ and with the word of God. I am that I am that I am the fullness of God and Satan fears me and trembles at my presence. In Jesus name I pray, Amen.

COVERING, PROTECTION & DELIVERANCE

In the name of Jesus Christ and by the power of Jesus blood, in the authority of Jesus word given to me as a child of God, I bind Satan. I command Satan to leave in Jesus' name. I seal this room, this house, this city, this state, this country and all the members of my family, relatives, friends and enemies and all our possessions, in the blood of Jesus Christ. I bind and reject all spirits. I bind all satanic forces. I loose the Holy Spirit in Jesus' name to take over and occupy every space that Satan has been evicted from. I bind and reject all spirits of confusion, all spirits of doubt, all spirits of disruption, all spirits of division, all spirits of deafness and dumbness, all spirits of disobedience, all spirits of games and all spirits of retaliation. I bind and reject all spirits of infirmity, all spirits of sickness and disease. I bind and reject all spirits of evil and death. I bind and reject all spirits of deception and error. I bind and reject the spirit of lie and ignorance and fear. I bind and reject all spirits of pride and arrogance. I bind and reject every sin of the spirit and the flesh. I bind and reject all spirits of hypocrisy in Jesus name. I bind and reject all spirits of distraction and command them to leave quietly without delay. I bind and reject all perverted spirits. I bind and reject Satan from my life and my family. I renounce Satan and all the forces of hell from my life and my family. I declare that Satan has no power over my life and my family. We love God and we serve the true and living God. I walk in God's perfect will for my life. I loose holiness, righteousness and godliness in my life. I loose the power of the Holy Spirit in my life. I loose Jesus Christ in my life. I loose God in my life. I loose joy, peace and happiness in my life. I loose health, healing, deliverance and restoration in my life. I loose greatness and newness in my life. I loose miracles, signs and wonders in my life. I loose truth, faith, the mind of Christ, hope, trust, humility, selflessness to Christ, submission to God's will and purpose for my life. I surrender all to Jesus. I surrender all to God. I surrender all to the Holy Spirit in my life. I declare God's will to be done in my life and not my will in Jesus name. I loose the spirit of wisdom, knowledge and understanding, the spirit of power and might in my life in Jesus name. I loose my mind on things above, on the kingdom of God, on things that are holy, pure, true, virtuous, honorable, just, kind, and good. I loose the eyes of my understanding to open up to see God's perfect plan for my life and his pathway for me to follow. I loose my hearing to hear only the voice of God my father, Jesus my brother and the Holy Spirit my comforter and teacher. In the name of Jesus Christ my Lord and Savior, I break and dissolve every curses, spells, hexes, evil wishes, evil desires and hereditary seals. I come against all satanic blood covenant, vows, powers, forces, pacts, satanic sacrifices and voodoo practices. I break and dissolve all links with psychics, clairvoyants, astrologers, mediums, occult seers, satanic cults, fortunetellers, séance, ouija board, tarot cards and occult games of all kinds. Come Holy Spirit of God and fill this vessel, this room, this house, this city, this state, this country and every area of my life with your presence and your power from corner to corner, ceiling to flooring, top to bottom and all around. I ask God in the name of Jesus Christ to loose all my angels to fight for my promises given unto me by God Almighty. This I ask in the name of my Lord and Savior Jesus Christ by the power of His blood, in the authority of God's written word given to me as a covenant child of promise from the Holy Bible. Lord Jesus, I ask today for an infilling of the Holy Spirit. Fill all the empty spaces within me with your peace, love, healing and joy, happiness and goodness. I ask for an increase and release of all the gifts and all the fruits and all the powers of the Holy Spirit. I thank you Lord for the word of knowledge, healing, miracles, wisdom, prophecy, faith, discernment of spirits, tongues, interpretation of tongues, deliverance, inner healing, teaching service, gifts of encouragement, gifts of leadership, gifts of preaching, gifts of joy and laughter; so that I may use all these gifts cheerfully for the glory of God. Father, you said to wait upon the Holy Spirit, he will come and give me power to be a witness unto you in all nations, so as I wait upon you, anoint me for ministry.

DELIVERANCE

Lord, bring salvation to the earth. Break the head of the sea monster. Destroy Leviathan the gliding sea serpent. Bring low the hills and the high mountains. Make straight the path of your righteousness in the midst of an evil and wicked generation. Uproot, cut down and break down all the great trees that does not bring you glory in the land. Put the sword to the priest who preaches lies and leads your people into hell and eternal damnation. Lay siege to the cities that rebel against you. Destroy man's idols. Smash, break down and destroy the idols of stones, silver, gold, wood and plastic, paper and cloth. Lift up your banner over the nations O Lord, God Almighty. Bring salvation by your own arm. Open the blind eyes and unstop the deaf ears. Cause the lame to walk and the dump to speak. Utterly destroy the God mammon. Take away the power of mammon to give wealth and riches to evil and wicked men. Bring trials and tribulation upon the evil and wicked people without ceasing. Take joy, peace, happiness, health, wealth, pleasure and power out of the hands of the evil and wicked men in Jesus name. Send the sword of judgment upon the heathens. Take their lands, their houses and all their wealth and possession and give to the poor. Give the wealth of the wicked to the righteous men and women of God. Take the treasures of darkness and give to the upright and just. Release the wealth of the wicked into the hands of the just. Plunder the evil and wicked who will not obey you. Break their covenants and packs and blood sacrifice with demons and everything evil and wicked. Make darkness light and cause the unrighteous nations, hills

17

and mountains and seas to stumble over the truth and be broken with God's rod of correction. Let the truth be exalted in all the earth and give your chosen power over all the works of their enemies. Make a road in mighty waters and a path way in the desert. Let the heathen fear God and his chosen. God, crush your foes and them that oppose you. Oppose them that oppose your word and utterly destroy the evil and wicked ones and cut off their generations. God, make a way of escape for me in every situation that would cause me harm or endanger my relationship with you in Jesus name. Amen.

DELIVERANCE FROM THE WICKED

Break the powers of the wicked and uphold the righteous mighty God. Bring down the wicked into corruption and lifts up the righteous in holiness. Let man fear and reverence God. Bring down the nations and cause my enemies to flee before me for you O God, have delivered me from death and my feet from stumbling. Be exalted, O God above the heavens and all the earth. My enemies have dug a pit for me and have set a net for my feet but instead they are snared by the works of their own hands. Break the bows and arrows of my enemies and blow them away like chaff in the wind. Break the teeth of my enemies and shatter their foundation. God, cause my enemies to wander about in darkness. Let the earth shake and open up to swallow the evil and wicked men that seeks the souls of your anointed. Bind and destroy the witches and the sorcerers. Confound and disillusion the wizards and the magicians. Lay waste to the plans, plots and schemes and works of all my enemies. Take away the peace of them that opposed and despised me, your anointed. God, posses the lands of my enemies and give it unto your anointed servant for your glory in Jesus name. Amen.

DELIVERANCE FROM ENEMIES

Kings and their army flee before God Almighty. The arms of the mighty are broken off. May those who desire to harm me flee with shame and utter disgrace. Let them slip, stumble and fall in their darkness and iniquity. Let their unrighteousness cease them with horror and utter dismay. Let their fruits, fail and the hands of their work glorify you O God or destroy the work of their hands. Let their own tongue be the weapon that destroys them. Let the evil they devise for others befall them with increase multiplicity. Let their nights be plague with misery and torment. Let their friends turn upon them and let their works stand against them. Wipe them off the face of the earth and sentence them to eternal death and damnation. Pluck them up out of the earth and cast them into hells fire. God, break the bows and shatters the spears of my enemy. God, destroy the shield of idols and the gods of this world. Heavenly Father, lay waste and destruction upon the idolatry of this people and this nation. Destroy the people who have no fear of you and have made void your laws and decrees. God, do not hold back your fist of destruction from this evil and perverse generation. They have removed you from the foundation of our society and have rejected and forgotten you, destroy them O Lord. For we shall worship only the true and living God and we shall put no other god before the Almighty, the only true God.

DELIVERANCE FROM THE WORKS OF THE ENEMY

May those who want to harm me become ashamed and disgraced. Destroy all those who hate God the father, Jesus the son and the Holy Spirit, the comforter in Jesus name. I am led by the spirit of God into all things. The people living in darkness have seen a great light. Repent all you people, nations and rulers, for the kingdom of heaven is at hand. Heal the minds, hearts and spirit of your people and let there be no feeble ones amongst the flock of God. Make the people of God strong and mighty upon the earth and cause their enemies to fear and flee before them. Cause the people of God to walk in boldness and authority over those that are not called by your name. Let our enemies scatter before us and let our blood brings forth life instead of the deaths of Christians. Let the spirit of Elisha come upon us when we face our enemies who attempt to take our lives. Let us prove you as the God with all power and let not Satan defeat us with premature deaths. We are the salt of the earth with the healing savor of God and the light of the world that cannot be hid. God has given me wisdom beyond my years into all things. All those who dishonor us shall suffer destruction as the kings who stole the Ark of the Covenant. God will make them that trespass against us to make financial restitution for their offences against God's anointed. Saul has slain his thousand and we will slay tens of thousand for God has given us the bear and the lion and God will give us Goliath's head. God in the name of Jesus, I ask you to destroy the spirit of pride and the spirit of stubbornness amongst your people.

DELIVERANCE FROM THE ENEMY'S DEFENSE

Every stone wall shall be broken down and every plastered stones shall crumble and fall. For the rock that the builder refused has become the head corner stone. For upon the rock of faith God has built his church. All those who reject the gospel of the good news shall be rejected from the earth that God has made for his glory. For God himself will make war with the inhabitant of the earth that will not serve or honor him. God will command the rain to cease from their land and caused the mighty waters to dry up. God will chase his enemies into the wilderness, where they will be utterly wasted. Those that fight against God's anointed servants fight against God. God will lay waste to all His enemies and erase their names from the earth. All who hear of God Almighty will fear him. Let God arise and let his enemies be scattered. All the plans of my enemies have failed. Confusion and distress are in the house of God's enemies. The pagans flee at the mention of the name of Jesus. The kingdom of darkness trembles at the sight and sound of me. This battle is not mines, it is the Lord. The Lord will fight for me and I will stand still and see the salvation of the Lord. Amen.

DELIVERANCE OF YOUR ENEMIES INTO YOUR HANDS

You come to me with a sword and a spear, but I come to you in the name of the Lord of the armies of heaven and of Israel, the very God whom you have defied. Today the Lord will conquer you and I will kill you and cut off your head; and then I will give the dead bodies of your army to the birds and wild animal, and the whole world will know that there is a God in this nation. God's people will learn that the Lord does not depend on weapons to fulfill his plans; he works without regards to human means. God will give us our enemies defeated while running for their lives. This day the Lord has delivered my enemies into my hands. And I will smite them and take their heads from them because they have challenged God by challenging me. God has brought down kings from their throne and has exalted me in humility. The prideful and arrogant has been brought down low even to the dust while God's anointed rule over them and inherit their wealth. Amen.

DELIVERANCE FOR GOD'S PEOPLE

God will save His people from the east, west, north and south. God will stand in the midst of His people and fight for them. God will loose His wrath against the enemies of His people. God will cut down, cut off and destroy His enemies and the enemies of His chosen. God has made His chosen into a warriors bow. He has used his chosen like sling shots and shoot us at His enemies. God's chosen will not plot evil against each other but they will speak the truth. Many people and powerful nation will come to seek me because God is with me. God will take away the silver and the gold from mammon and his patrons and give to his anointed. God will take away their homes and their possession and give unto his anointed. Because the wealth of the wicked are stored up for the just and God has given the heathen travail to heap up wealth for the righteous. God will cut you down O Greece. God will cut Greece down and utterly destroy her kings and her princes and strongman over the nations where she has spread herself. Never will an oppressor overrun God's people for He now stand watch and declares freedom, peace, and prosperity for his people. God's arrows will flash like lightening and destroy our enemies, the princes, the kings and the rulers of darkness. God will remove and utterly destroy every evil and wicked rulers and leaders in his house. God will cut off and bring destruction upon the prophets of Baal and the false teachers and false pastors. Woe to the false shepherds of idols, the sword shall be upon his arm and upon his right eye. His arm shall dry up and his right eye shall be darkened. God will cut off the names of idols out of the land, and they shall no more be remembered and God will cause the false prophets and the unclean spirits to pass out of the land. The false prophets that prophesy lies in the name of the Lord God Almighty shall be put to death by his own mouth and shall be no more. Awake O sword of the Lord and smite the evil and wicked, lying false shepherds. They will build but the Lord will demolish and tear down that which he has not spoken. God's name will be great amongst the nations. God is a great king and his name is to be feared. God will judge all the priest, prophets and teachers according to his word and render his judgment. Lord cut off them that are married to foreign gods. God send the refiners fire upon the earth to purge away the wicked. They that feared the Lord shall live. God will separate the righteous from the wicked. The righteous will trample down the wicked under their feet. Amen.

DELIVERANCE FROM EVIL MEN

Prepare for war; let all the fighting men come near for God has declared war upon the inhabitant of the earth. The Lord roars from mount Zion and thunder from the high mountains. God will break down the gates of the heathens and the bars of the rebellious. I will cut off the people who rejects me saith the Lord. God will send fire on the walls of the prideful and arrogant ones. God will not keep back his punishment from the nation that curse and laugh at him from there low places. God will pull down the nation's stronghold and their gods. God will destroy the alters of idols. God will break the arms and legs of the diviners, the prophets and the priests of Baal. God will send plagues upon them that hate him. God will kill the first born of them that oppress his people and dishonor his name. But in my wrath if you seek me, you will live but if you turn from the Lord in his anger, the Lord will bring destruction and ruin upon you. Your wealth and your pride have caused you to reject God and have oppressed his anointed, because of this you will not live in the houses you have built or enjoy the fruits of your labor but your servant shall inhabit your homes and spend the fruits of your labor. Justice will prevail. The Lord God Almighty declares that the rich who forgets the ways of the Lord shall be poor and banished into exile because they forget the Lord's word and counsel. God will command his sword to slay his enemies and set his eyes upon the evil and wicked one for evil and not good. God will punish those who use their wealth and power to do hateful wickedness against God and his anointed. Amen.

DELIVERANCE POWER

Arise O daughter of the Most High God and thresh the nations for God has given you horns of steel and feet of iron. Run upon the mighty giants and trample them down under your feet. God has given me all power over my enemies and the works and the plans of Satan against me have failed. God has given me the lion and God has given me the bear and God will give me Goliath. God has anointed me to slay giants and bring deliverance to nations and kingdoms. Amen.

DELIVERANCE FOR GOD'S ANOINTED

God send your angels with swords drawn to oppose my enemies. Let the angels of the Lord stand in the pathways of my enemies and discomfort them. God in the name of Jesus let no man put a curse on me or my family. God in the name of Jesus let no false prophet; false preacher and false apostle speak into my life. Shut the mouth of my enemies and open their eyes to see the angels of the Lord that you have assigned me to discomfort them with their swords armed. Silenced the tongue of the curser and open the mouths of the blessed to bless me and my family without ceasing. God let nobody curse me because I am blessed. Send the angles of the Lord to remove or destroy all whom desire to hurt or destroy me in Jesus name. Make me and my family too powerful for our enemies to attack or overthrow. Open my eyes to see your warring angels that you have assigned me. Open the eyes of my enemies to see the warring angels that God has assigned me. Father God, destroy them that pays a fee for divination and destroy the prophets that divines for profit. Send the angel of the Lord to destroy them. No one can curse who God has not curse or denounce who God has not denounced. Bless all my enemies in Jesus name. God is not a man that He should lie or the son of man that He should repent; shall God promise and not bring it to pass? Does God speak and not act. The Lord God is with me. The Lord brought me up out of bondage. The shout of God is in my mouth and a double hedge sword in my hand. God has put his oracles in my mouth and I speak with great wisdom, knowledge and understanding. My learning exceeds that of my peers because of the divine revelation of the Holy Spirit, my teacher, who teaches me all truth. I speak with holy boldness and fear no evil for God is with me and what he command me to say I speak without fear. I have commanded blessings in my life and it is so. Therefore, no sorcery can prevent me, God's anointed from accomplishing my task. There is no divination against God's anointed. The workers of witchcraft and iniquity that rises up against me shall perish. The land shall open up and swallow them up for touching God's anointed. I rise like a lioness. I rose myself like a lion to devour my prey. For God has put a message in my mouth and I speak. I have the strength of a wild ox. God has blessed me and none can reverse God's blessing upon my life. Let the spirit of God come upon me. God is exalted in all my life. I fear God with all reverence and know that the fear of God protects me from false teaching and doctrines. God will always deliver me because I am his servant and his ears are open unto me. When I call, God will hear and answer me because I am his anointed child.

DELIVERANCE OF POSSESSIONS

Go into all the land that I have given you and dispossess the people and nations greater and stronger than you. God will subdue and drive out the people from before me. Because of the wickedness of these nations the Lord is driving out the people from before me. The Lord will go ahead of me like a devouring fire and no one will be able to stand against me for God shall destroy them. Amen.

DELIVERANCE OF THE RIGHTEOUS

The desires of the righteous shall be granted. The foot of the righteous shall not be removed. The righteous shall inherit the earth. The way of the righteous is made plain. Surely as I have thought so shall it come to pass and as I have purposed so shall it stand. For the Lord of hosts hath purposed, and who shall disannul it? And his hand is stretched out, and who shall turn it back? It shall come to pass within three years. Your enemies are dead, they shall not live, and they are deceased. They shall not rise for the Lord has visited them and destroyed them. Seek you out of the book of the Lord and read: not one of God's promises to me shall fail, none shall want her mate: for my mouth it is commanded, and his spirit it has gathered them. Every valley shall be exalted and every mountain and hill shall be made low. The crooked shall be made straight and the rough places plain. They that wait upon the Lord shall renew their strength. They shall mount up with wings as eagles. They shall run and not be weary; and they shall walk, and not faint. The Lord put forth his hand, and touched my mouth. And the Lord said unto me behold I have put my words in thy mouth. The word of the Lord came to me telling me what to say. I will hasten my word to perform it. For behold I have made thee this day a defended city, and an iron pillar, and brazen walls against the kings of Judah, against the princes thereof against the priest thereof and against the people of the land. Amen.

DELIVERANCE IN THE DANCE

Let me praise God's name in the dance, to execute vengeance upon the heathen, and punishments upon the people; to bind their kings with chains, and their nobles with fetters of iron. For by God, I have run through a troop and by my God, have I leaped over a wall. He makes my feet like hinds feet, and sets me upon my high places. God teaches my hands to war, so that a bow of steel is broken by mine arms. I have pursued mine enemies, and overtaken them; neither did I turn again till they were consumed. Great deliverance gives God to his king, and shows mercy to his anointed, to me and to my seed for evermore. And the God of peace shall bruise Satan under my feet right now. God has given me power in the dance to destroy the works of Satan and the kingdom of darkness. God has given me the gift of spontaneous warfare dance. I dance and war for souls, healing, deliverance, anointing and the power of God. I wave the weapons of my warfare to cast out demons and evil spirit from churches, cities, nations and families. When I feel oppressive or evil spirit in the church, home and around someone, I praise dance and warfare dance until a lifting or deliverance takes place.

28

I dance to bring breakthroughs in every area of ones life and ministry. I have wounded my enemies that they were not able to rise, they are fallen under my feet. God has girded me with strength unto the battle. God subdued under me those that rose up against me. Then did I beat them small as the dust before the wind. I did cast them out as the dirt in the streets. I arise with boldness and strength, for the joy of the Lord is my strength. Before, I entered the battle the deliverance of the Lord was granted unto me, so let it be as it is written. My enemies are defeated and they flee in terror and fear, for the dread of me is upon them; because, the Lord fights all my battles and gives me the victory. Amen.

DELIVERANCE FROM FOES

For by thee I have run through a troop; and by my God have I leaped over a wall. It is God that girds me with strength, and makes my way perfect. He makes my feet like hinds feet and set me upon my high places. God teaches my hands to war so that a bow of steel is broken by mine arms. God has given me the shield of His salvation. And God's right hand is holding me up, and His gentleness has made me great. God has enlarged my steps under me so that my feet did not slip. I have pursued my enemies and overtaken them. I did not turn until all my enemies were consumed. I have wounded my enemies and they are not able to rise up against me anymore. My foes are fallen under my feet. For the Lord has girded me with strength unto the battle. God has subdued under me those that rose up against me. God has also given me the necks of mine enemies that I might destroy them that hate me. Thou hast delivered me form the striving of the people and thou hast made me the head of the heathen and a people whom I have not known shall serve me. God delivers me from mine enemies. God lifts me up above those that rise up against me. God has delivered me from the violent man. The Lord is my shepherd, I shall not want. God prepares a table before me in the presence of mine enemies. God anoints my head with oil; my cup runs over. Deliver me from the workers of iniquity, and save me from bloody men. They have prepared a net for my steps. They have dug a pit before me, into the midst whereof they are fallen themselves. Jesus has ascended on high and has led captivity captive. I have received gifts for men and all the horns of the wicked will I cut off and exalt the horns of the righteous. I will beat down his foes before his face and plague them that hate God. The Lord shall deliver me from the snare of the fowler, and from the noisome pestilence. A thousand shall fall dead at my side and ten thousand at my right hand but it shall not come near me. There shall no evil befall me neither shall any plague come near my dwelling. I will tread upon lions and adders but the young lion and the dragon shall I trample under my feet. God suffered no man to do me harm. God rebuked kings for my sake because it is written touch not my anointed and do my prophets no harm. With my lips, I declare all the judgment of the Lord. Establish your word unto me Mighty God. And remember the words that you have spoken unto me, which has caused me to hope. Heavenly Father, bring your words to pass in Jesus name. I believe it is time for the Lord to bring his words to pass in my life because the people have made void your laws and have rejected you. Order my steps in your word O God and let not any iniquity have dominion over me. Deliver me from the oppression of man. Surely the Lord will slay the wicked. Depart from me therefore, you bloody men. Keep me O Lord, from the hands of the wicked and violent man. Preserve me from the violent men, who have purposed to overthrow my goings. Evil shall hunt the violent man to overthrow him. Cut off my enemies and destroy them all that afflict my soul for I am thy anointed servant. The Lord shall build up Zion and appear in His glory. Blessed be the Lord my strength which teach my hands to war, and my fingers to fight. The Lord preserves them that love Him but all the wicked will He destroy. The way of the wicked the Lord turns upside down. The Lord cast the wicked down to the ground. His word runs very swiftly. The Lord has made a decree which shall come to pass. For it is written let not a witch live. Remove the workers of iniquity far from me and I decree the fire of God to fall on every evil and wicked works of my enemies. God utterly destroy the works of wickedness in Jesus name. Amen.

PROTECTION

The Lord is my refuge and my fortress. My God in him I will trust. He shall deliver me from the snare of the fowler, and from the noisome pestilence. The Lord shall cover me with his feathers, and under his wings shall I trust. God's word shall be my shield and buckler. I shall not be afraid for the terror by night. Nor for the arrow that flies by day. Nor for the pestilence that walks in darkness, nor for the destruction that wasted at noonday. A thousand shall fall at my side and ten thousand at my right hand; but it shall not come near me. There shall no evil befall me and my seed neither shall any plague, sickness, diseases or infirmities come near my home. God shall give his angels charge over me to keep me in all my ways. I will tread upon Satan, witchcraft, evil spirits and all the works of mine enemies. God will deliver me from all harm and danger and set me on high, above all my peers and enemies. Amen.

PROTECTION FROM EVIL

God, I am your servant. Save me and deliver me from all my enemies and my foes. Preserve me in righteousness and keep me steadfast in your laws. Keep me perfect before you and uphold me with your righteous right hand. Protect me and deliver me from the kingdom of darkness. Send your holy warring angels to guard and protect me from the princes of the air, the spiritual wickedness in high places, the rulers of darkness, and the powers of satanic and demonic spirits. Cancel and destroy all works of evil and wickedness towards me from foe or friend. Let the glory of the Lord be revealed in me for truly I am God's servant. Protect my family and all my possession from every attack of the enemy. Mighty God of War utterly cast down and destroy the souls of Satanist that seeks to destroy me by means of witchcraft, evil and wick devices conceived by Satan. When the spiritual force of darkness attacks me let the avenging angels of God engage them in battle to utter destruction and guard me with your presence.

PROTECTION FROM ENEMIES

Protect me and hide me from evil man. Let me stand under the banner of the Lord of righteousness. Utterly waste and destroy them that would rise against me. Let all your plans for my life be established and proceed on course without delay. Give me rest and peace from all my enemies. Render the prayers of the wicked null and void and of no effects. Cause confusion and utter destruction in the enemy's camp. Lay siege to the cities of this nation and rip it from the gripped of the evil ones. Shoot down the principalities with your powerful bow O Mighty God of war. Tear down the defense of my enemies from around them and give me their land for a possession in Jesus name. Crush all the heads of all your enemies O God. Break the heads of the idols. Break the arms and legs of their graven images and bring them to the dust. Scatter your foes into utter darkness. Bind the princes with chains and fretter of iron. Bring down the strongmen over your people to everlasting ruin. Confused the wicked and confound their minds. Bring down the wicked into the pit of corruption. Let their curses and lies consume them. Father, in the name of Jesus I command the mouth of the liars to be silent. Amen.

PROTECTION FROM FEAR

When I am afraid, I will trust in God. I will not fear man because what can they do to my soul? Have mercy on me God and cover me with the blood of Jesus Christ and hedge me in with your word of protection. Let no harm befall me and let no evil come near me or my dwelling. Destroy the rulers of evil and wickedness. Mighty God, rule over the earth with power and authority for you are Lord, King and God of all creation. Make deposit into the kingdom of God and take withdrawal out of the kingdom of darkness. Consume the wealth of the wicked and bring them to poverty and disgrace. Bring the waves upon the land and clean the hills and mountains of the blood that still cries out to you for justice. Vomit up the evil and wicked men from off the land. Open the earth and swallow up the rebellious and greedy people. Put the god mammon in chains and fretters of iron and cast him into prison for his pride and acts against you O Mighty God. Crush the heads of your enemies and cast their crowns to the ground. Let the pit close its mouth over my enemies. God, rebuild the city and cause the children of servants to live in the land for your glory and honor. Amen.

PROTECTION FROM EVIL PLANS

Mighty God of war, I ask in the name of Jesus for your protection from all the plans and wiles of the devil. God in the name of Jesus please hedge me in and around with your word and the blood of Jesus Christ. Lord, let your will be done in my life and establish all your plans for me and my family without delays. Lord God, take charge of my life in every area and guide me into heaven. Let my child walk before you pure and holy. Lord, destroy all the plans of my enemies and the enemies of my family and ministry. Let your word surround me like a flaming fire. Send angels to watch and protect me from all danger. Let the sword of God proceed from my mouth and cut down all my enemies. Awesome God, fill the whole earth with your glory. Show me your glory God. Show the earth the glory of God. Lord, show mighty signs and wonders upon the earth through my hands. Heal the sick, raise the dead and cast out demons in the name of Jesus that men may see, know and fear you for your greatness. Lord, God create righteousness in all the earth and rain righteousness upon the earth. Pour righteousness upon the people. Let salvation cover the earth and the atmospheres. Amen.

PROTECTION FROM THE BLOOD

Mighty God, I boldly confess your word unto you in the name of your beloved son Jesus Christ. I am covered in the blood of Jesus and apply the blood of Jesus to my entire life and family. I walk by faith and not by sight therefore I am not moved by what I see but by the words of God. I walk in divine healing and health. I have whatsoever I say according to the word of God. I have the power of life and death in my tongue and I command life in every area of my life, ministry, family and business. Lord, fill me with your glory and let the radiance of your presence over whelm me in Jesus name. God in the name of Jesus bring back your glory to my temple and to my home and to my body. God send me your glory. God bring me into your glory and glorify me with the glory I had before the world was. Father God, in the name of Jesus manifest your presence unto me for I am thirsty for you and boldly come before your throne to seek your face continually. God, you said if I seek you with my whole heart I would find you, where are you God?

PROTECTION EDGING

I declare that God has made an edge of protection around me and around my house and around everything that I have on every side and around my family, my job, my business and my church in Jesus name. I cancel the plans of all my enemies in Jesus name. I render Satan and his powers null and void in my life in Jesus name. I break every satanic and demonic strongholds in my life in the name of Jesus. I break every generational and every ancestral curse from my life and linage right now in the name of Jesus. I bind up every curse sent against me and my family in the name of Jesus. I loose the blessings of God in my life and my families' life in the name of Jesus. I cancel out every evil and wicked works against me in the name of Jesus. I decree and declare that God has blessed the work of my hands and caused craft to prosper in my hand with witty ideas and new inventions in Jesus name. Amen.

PROTECTION AND DELIVERANCE FOR COUPLES

I have given help to my chosen and anointed servants. I have anointed them with holy oil. My strength will always be with them. My power will make them strong. Their enemies will never succeed against them. The wicked will not defeat them. God will crush our foes and remove everyone who hates us. God will make us always victorious. God will always keep his promise to us and God's covenant with us will last forever. God will not stop loving us or fail to have mercy upon us. God will not break his covenant with us or take back even one promise He has made us. God will never lie to us because God cannot lie. He will watch over his words to bring them to pass. God, you are our defender and protector. You are our God; in you we trust. God will keep us safe from all hidden dangers and from all deadly disease. A thousand shall fall dead beside us and ten thousand all around us but we will not be harmed. We will look and see how the Lord punishes our enemies and the wicked. The Lord is our defender and protector. No disaster will strike us; no violence will come near our homes. God has placed his warring angels in charge of us to protect us wherever we go. The warring angels will hold us up with their hands to keep us from hurting our feet on the stone. We will trample down lions and snakes, fierce lions and poisonous snakes. When we call to the Lord he will answer us. The Lord will rescue and honor us. Lord, you give us rest from our days of trouble. Fire goes in front and around us to burn up our enemies. Lord, rescue us from the powers of the wicked. Bring our marriage fulfillment and let nothing or no one put asunder what you have joined together. Keep my husband before your face Lord and give him favor because it is written that a man who finds a wife finds a virtuous woman and obtains favor from the Lord. Remove every obstacle and every force that would prevent us from coming together in unity. As we are joined in the spirit join us in the natural and bring us on one accord in agreement with each other. God turn us to face each other with great love and desire for each other. Bind us with the cords of our marriage vows and loose us from separation and division. Increase our intimate time with each other and keep us together. Teach us to worship and praise you together as one and strengthen us as we pray together daily. Keep us on the right track and cancel all plans, works and tricks of the enemy in our lives. Remove, cancel and destroy every work of witchcraft that has been sent against us. Remove every person or persons from our life that are hindering our relationship with each other. Seal us with your blood and cover us in your robe of righteousness. Let all our enemies be scattered and consumed with fire. Bring us into unity and agreement with each other. Turn situations in our favor. Block all interference and destroy every weapon and every work of the enemy. Take us from the midst of oppression and place us on our mountaintop together to reign in victory. Give us what is ours and give our enemies what is theirs. The evil that was meant for us turn it into a blessing. Deliver us from our enemies that are too strong for us. Remove, stop, destroy and disable all our enemies that rise up against us. Bless us for the attacks of the enemies with favor. Cement us together all the days of our life and make us one. Make us strong together, like mighty warriors. Give us power to operate in the freedom of miraculous powers. Give us the powers to overcome our adversity. Deliver us Lord God Almighty. Deliver us from sin and death. Deliver us from our enemies and friends who hate us. Deliver us into freedom and victory. Cause our paths before us to shine and our ways to be perfect before God. Let your word be a lamp unto our feet and paths for us to walk upon all the days of our lives. Let the glory of God be revealed and magnified upon us to bring us into unity together and in love. To God, be all the glory and honor in Jesus name. Amen.

WITCHCRAFT AND ENEMIES

God's hand will lay hold of all my enemies. The Lord will bring all the works of evil doers to nothing. The right hand of God will capture my enemies. In your wrath O Mighty God you will swallow up my enemies, in your consuming fire. Their descendants will be destroyed from the earth and their names forgotten. They that plot evil against me and wicked schemes will fail for the Lord is my stay. The Lord has given me great joy in victory over all my enemies and my foes. God has turned every curse into a blessing and multiplied the sorrows of mine enemies. They that tried to destroy me are no more for the Lord has laid hold to them. I am God's anointed and God's prophet and my God will avenge me. My enemies will not prosper in their device to do evil against me for God sees all and hears all. Nothing that is done in secret is hidden from the eyes of God for he does not slumber nor sleep. The powers of darkness have no powers over me. The principalities, rulers of darkness and spiritual wickedness in high places are under my feet for God has given me dominion over the works of Satan upon the earth. Lord you will cast down my enemies into their own traps, who have dug a hole to devour me. Lord heap coals of fire upon their heads and cause their own works to judge against them. I am free from all the tricks, deceits anger, envy and jealousy of my enemies. I rise high and mightily above those that prosecutes me and tries to destroy me. For it is written that no weapons formed against me shall prosper. That every tongue that rises in judgment against me I have the power to condemn in Jesus name. It is also written that I should not suffer a witch to live; so by the power vested in me by the Almighty God I declare death by fire to every witch that rises up against me to destroy me or to come against me in anyway, shape or fashion unless they turn from their wicked ways and repent. I declare that God will burn all the witches that rises up against the children of God, the moment they propose iniquity in their heart, unless they repent and turn from their wicked ways. As Elijah calls fire from heaven to consume the sacrifice to defeat Baal prophets, so call I fire from heaven to consume all the false prophets and workers of witchcraft. As Elisha calls fire from heaven to consume his enemies, so call I fire from heaven to consume the witch doctors, warlocks, satanic cults, diviners and psychics of all sorts. As God forbids Balaam to curse Israel so has God prevented the workers of witchcraft to curse me. God will turn all curses sent against me into blessings and the witches shall perish for touching God's anointed. Therefore, I pray for their deliverance and repentance in Jesus name. Amen.

TO FORGIVE YOUR ENEMIES

Dearest God, heal me of my pain and hurt which was caused by my enemies. Teach me how to love and forgive my enemies for the evil they have wished me and the destruction they have released upon me. God will repay them that hate me to their face, God will not be slack to them that hate me. He will repay them to their face. Teach me your ways O Lord. Let me know that you will avenge me because vengeance belongs to you. Lord, I thank you that everything will work for my good, because I love you. I recognize every attack of the enemy as an opportunity for a blessing, by removing iniquity from my heart. I thank you Lord that you have allowed the enemy to attack so you can purify me and perfect my praise unto you and prove what is in my heart. Give ear to my words O Lord and bring your words for my life to pass. Teach me how to wait on you without murmuring and doubting your abilities to deliver me in times of trouble. Cause me to rise above my enemies let not my foot slip from your pathway to my destiny. Remove the obstacles setup by my enemies and teach me how to pray blessings upon their lives instead of curses. Let not mine enemies prevail against me, but cause me to prevail against them because you are my God and you defend me with your right arm. How can my enemy prevail against me when God is my strong tower and my house of defense? Has anyone prevailed against the true and living God? Is there a contender for my God? Who dare stand against my God? Not Satan or his army for God is too powerful to contend with in battle because there is none to deliver out of his hands. Turn curses sent against me into many blessings. Almighty God, bless and prosper my enemies in every good works. Save and deliver them from death and destruction. Cause them to see their errors and lead them into repentance. Lord because you have forgiven my enemies of their sin and trespass against me, I have forgiven them of their sins and trespasses against me. For as I have forgiven those that trespass against me so have you forgiven me of my sins. Heal me now O Lord that I can testify of your goodness and mercy towards me. Show me your loving kindness and bless me with your peace that surpasses all understanding in Jesus name.

ENVY AND JEALOUSY

How good God is to Israel to those whose hearts are pure. But as for me, I came so close to the edge of the cliff! My feet were slipping and I was almost gone; because, I was envious of the prosperity of the proud and the wicked. Yes, all through life their road is smooth! They grow sleek and fat. They aren't always in trouble and plagued with problems like everyone else, so their pride sparkles like a jeweled necklace, and their clothing is woven of cruelty. These fat cats have everything their hearts could ever wish for. They scoff at God and threaten his people. How proudly they speak! They boast against the very heavens, and their words shout through the earth. And so God's people are dismayed and confused, and drink it all in. Does God realize what is going on they ask? Look at these men of arrogance; they never have to lift a finger, theirs is a life of ease; and all the time their riches multiply." Have I been wasting my time? Why take the trouble to be pure? All I get out of it is trouble and woe every day and all day long' If I had really said that, I would have been a traitor to your people. Yet it is so hard to explain it, this prosperity of those who hate the Lord. Then one day I went into God's sanctuary to mediate, and thought about the future of these evil men. What a slippery path they are on, suddenly God will send them sliding over the edge of the cliff and down to their destruction: an instant end to all their happiness, an eternity of terror. Their present life is only a dream. They will awaken to the truth as one awakens from a dream of things that never really were. When I saw this, what turmoil filled my heart! I saw myself so stupid and so ignorant; I must seem like an animal to you, O God. But even so, you love me. You are holding my right hand. You will keep on guiding me all my life with your wisdom and counsel; and afterwards receive me into the glories of heaven. Who have I in heaven but you? And I desire no one on earth as much as God. My health fails; my spirits droop, yet God remains. He is the strength of my heart; he is mines forever. But those refusing to worship God will perish, for he destroys those serving other gods. But as for me, I get as close to him as I can: I have chosen him and I will tell everyone about the wonderful ways he rescues me. Amen.

WARFARE AND JUDGMENT

Woe unto the false teachers, the false prophets and the false pastors because God has risen up against them and destroyed them. Satan's kingdom has fallen. Babylon has fallen. Greece has fallen. Rome has fallen and shall never rise again. The enemies of God flee from their hiding place of rest for the arrows of God pursue them to utter destruction. The spirit of death and the spirit of destruction obeys the voice of God. Death and destruction consumes them that rise up against me and the kingdom of God. The gods of this world has left their abode fleeing for their life while the angels of God pursue them and utterly destroy them. The end has come and the sons and daughters of God has been revealed. No weapons form by man or spirit shall prosper against me. I am hedge in with the protection of God. No harm shall befall me and no evil shall come near me. Those that rise up against me fall by the hundreds, by the thousands, and by the tens of hundred thousands because God has given his angels charge over me to keep me in all my ways. The Lord fight against them that fight against me and has laid hold of all my enemies for greater is the Holy Spirit in me than Satan in the world. There are more with me than them against me. Amen.

WARFARE STONED WALLS

Not one stone on another shall be left here but everyone will be torn down. Come to Jesus a living stone and like a living stone, let yourself be built into a spiritual house, to be a holy priesthood, to offer spiritual sacrifices acceptable to God through Christ. God has laid a stone in Zion. The stone the builder refused has become the head corner stones. Jesus is the stone that will make the unrighteous stumble and He is the rock of faith that makes the unbelievers fall. Those that disobey the word of God shall stumble and fall for God shall judge the wicked now. God has cut a rock with his hands out of the mountain and has sailed the rock at the images of idols and statues. The statues of iron, clay, bronze, silver and gold are broken to pieces and become chaff in the wind. The wind blows them away without leaving a trace and the rock has become a great mountain and fills the earth. God will stone all his enemies and the gods of the heathens from heaven. He will rain fire and brimstones upon the inhabitants of the city that will not serve him. God will trample down all the idols under his feet and will crush the god's of this world.
Light will shine in darkness and a way of holiness shall be exalted in all the earth. The army of God shall devour, and subdue their enemy with sling stones. Behold the stone that I have laid before Joshua, upon

one stone shall be seven eyes: I will remove the iniquity of that land in one day. Behold this stone shall be a witness unto him for whosoever shall fall on this stone shall be broken: but on whomever it shall fall it will grind him to powder. God will rain stones from heaven killing all his enemies that fights against his bride and anointed servant. I cast a stone bind with the word of God into the midst of the river and I declare thus Babylon shall sink. A tried stone is laid in Zion for a foundation. On every land I cast the stone with the word of God that shall never fail nor return unto God void but shall accomplish that which it is sent out to do. The laws of God are written in stones. Thou the stone may be broken the word can never fail. The word of God stands forever for God rules the world forever and ever and ever. Amen.

WARFARE THE GREAT TREES

All the trees of the field are withered and the flames have burned all the trees of the field. Cut down the tree, and cut off his branches, shake off his leaves, and scatter his fruits; let the beasts get away from under it, and the fowls from his branches. Cut the tree down and destroy it. All the trees of the field shall know that I the Lord have brought down the high trees and have exalted the low tree, have dried up the green tree, and have make the dry tree to flourish. I the Lord have spoken and have done it. Let no fruit grow on the trees of the forest for ever. God will send condemnation and rain fire upon them that make sacrifice under trees and unto trees. God will kindle fire in thee, and shall devour every green tree in thee, and every dry tree. The flaming flame shall not be quenched, and all faces from south to north and east to west shall be burned therein. All thy trees and fruits of thy land shall the locust consume. And God shall smite every fenced city and every choice city, and every good tree shall fall and stop all wells of water and mar every good piece of land with stones. Fall all the good trees. Let us destroy the trees with their fruits of our enemies. None of the trees of this land shall yield their fruits; for the axe is laid unto the root of the trees and every tree that does not bring good fruit it will be cut down and cast into the fire. God smote the fig trees and break the trees of their coast. Under every green tree where they offer to idols shall the sword of judgment fall upon their houses and the houses of their children. Scream fir tree for the cedar is fallen, because the mighty are spoiled. Howl you oak trees of Bashan, for the forest of the vintage has come down and your glory has become your shame. Your pride has been brought low and you have been struck with the fist of God. Your god's are scattered and flee before the Lord God Almighty and his servants. The sword of God will come against this nation and put an end to Satan's kingdom in this place this very moment without delay for God has honored the words of his prophets who are his mouth piece. Amen.

DECLARATION TO SATAN

Son of man say unto Satan, saith the Sovereign Lord: You were the model of perfection, full of wisdom and perfect in beauty. You were in the Garden of Eden; every precious stone adorned you: You were anointed as a guardian cherub, for so I ordained you. You were on the holy mount of God; you walked among the fiery stones. You were blameless in your ways from the day you were created till wickedness was found in you. Through your widespread trade, you were filled with violence, and you sinned. So I drove you in disgrace from the mount of God, and I expelled you. O guardian cherub, your heart became proud on account of your beauty, and you corrupted your wisdom because of your splendor. So I threw you to the earth; I made a spectacle of you before kings. By your many sins and dishonest trade you have desecrated your sanctuaries. So I made a fire come out from you and it consumed you. And I reduced you to ashes on the ground in the sight of all who were watching. All the nations who knew you are appalled at you; you have come to a horrible end and will be no more. The weapons we fight with are not the weapons of the world. They have divine power to demolish strongholds. We demolish arguments and every pretension that sets itself up against the knowledge of God, and we take captive every thought to make it obedient to Christ. Satan you have fallen from heaven, Lucifer, son of the morning! You are cut down to the ground. For thou hast said in your heart, I will ascend into heaven, I will exalt my throne above the stars of God: I will sit also upon the mount of the congregation, in the sides of the north" I will ascend above the heights of the clouds: I will be like the most High. Yet Satan shall be brought down to hell, to the sides of the pit. And the Lord said unto Satan, The Lord rebuke thee, O Satan; even the Lord that hath chosen Jerusalem rebuke thee: is not this a brand plucked out of the fire? Get thee behind me, Satan: thou art an offence unto me.

PRACTICE NO EVIL

When you enter the land the Lord your God is giving you, do not learn to imitate the detestable ways of the nations there. Let no one be found among you who sacrifices his son or daughter in the fire, who practices divination or sorcery, interprets omens, engages in witchcraft, or cast spells, or who is a medium or spiritist or who consults the dead. Anyone who does these things is detestable to the Lord, and because of these detestable practices the Lord your God will drive out those nations before you. You must be blames before the Lord your God. The nations you will dispossess listen to those who practice sorcery or divination. But as for you, the Lord your God has not permitted you to do so. The Lord will raise up a prophet like me from among your own brothers. You must listen to him. Amen.

THE WRATH OF GOD

God's reputation is very great in cities and in nations. His home is in Jerusalem. He lives upon Mount Zion. There he breaks the weapons of our enemies. The everlasting mountains cannot compare with you in glory. The mightiest of our enemies are conquered. They lie before us in the sleep of death: not one can lift a hand against us. When you rebuked them, God of my forefather and my God, steeds and riders fell. No wonder you are greatly feared. Who can stand before an angry God? You pronounce sentence on them from heaven; the earth trembles and stand silently before you. You stand up to punish the evil doers and to defend the meek of the earth. Fulfill all your vows that you have made to Jehovah your God. Let everyone bring him presents. He should be reverenced and feared, for he cuts down princes and does awesome things to the kings of the earth.

POSSESSING OUR POSSESSION

God has commanded me to take possession of the land He has given me for an inheritance. God has declared the boundaries of my land for the possession. God has established my boundaries on the east. God has established my boundaries on the west. God has established my boundaries on the north. God has established my boundaries on the south. God has commanded my enemies to give up my land and flee to utter darkness. God has built himself as my stronghold in the midst of the land He has given unto me. God dwells with me. God has given unto me and Abraham, Isaac and Jacob land. God has promised me land as heir of Abraham for his faith and trust in God-(Faithfulness). God has given me this land. God will give me the land I set my feet on and have spied out for the possession. The Lord my God has blessed me in all the work of my hand and in all my life I have not lacked anything. This very day I will put the fear and dread of you in all the nations. God is delivering my enemies and their land into my hands. I have began conquering and possessing the land of my enemies. God has given into my hands the enemies and their entire armies. I have secured all the towns, cities and nations God has given unto me. The Lord, God himself will fight for me. God is my shield and my great reward; therefore, I will not fear. I will walk the land that God has given to me and my generation for the possession in the breath and length. God has given me all the lands I can see in the east, the west, the north and the south for the possession. The land of promise is mines. God has given me and my generation the land flowing with milk and honey. God has discomforted my enemies from off my land and have caused me to possess the land without money. I live on lands I did not purchase. I will live in houses I did not build. I will own goodly furniture that I did not purchase. I will receive the wealth of the wicked. I will eat the labor of the gentiles. I will rule over the heathens for my inheritance. God has given me the heathen for my inheritance. The wealth of the wicked are stored up for the righteous. I reap where I have not sown. I have become great and a powerful nation. The nations fear me because of what the Lord has done for me. I have no lack. I have abundance. I am healthy, wealthy and wise. I have prosperity. I am prosperous. I have whatsoever I say. These words that I speak are life. These words I speak are the words of God. These words I speak shall never fail but shall be established and come to pass quickly for they are fast and sharp. I think and say that I am God's child and I am becoming more like God every day of my life. I am walking like God, my father. I am talking like God, my father. I and my father is one. I am one with God. I am unified with God. I am doing my father's business. What I see God do, I do. What I hear God say, I say. I act like God and speak like God and I am able to create God's kingdom on earth. God's will is done in me. I walk in the fullness of God: I am like God and where God leads me I will follow him without resistance. Amen.

PRESIDENT AND LEADERS

O God, help the president to judge as you would, and help his children to walk in godliness. Help him to give justice to your people, even to the poor. May the mountains and hills flourish in prosperity because of his good reign. Help him to defend the poor and the needy and to crush their oppressors. May the poor and the needy revere you constantly, as long as sun and moon continues in the skies. Yes, forever! May the reign of this President be as gentle and fruitful as the springtime rain upon the grass, like showers that water the earth. May all good men flourish in his reign, with abundance of peace to the end of time. Let him reign from sea to sea and from the river of life to the ends of the earth. The desert nomads shall bow before him; his enemies shall fall face downward in the dust. Kings along the Mediterranean coast, the kings of nations and the island, and those from Asia and Europe, all will bring their gifts. Yes, kings from everywhere, all will bow before him, all will serve him. He will take care of the helpless and the poor when they cry to him; for they have no one else to defend them. He feels pity for the weak and needy, and will rescue them. He will save them from oppression and from violence, for their lives are precious to him. And he shall live; and to him will be given the gold of the nations, and there will be constant praise for him; because, God has given him for a witness and a great leader of the people. God go before our leaders by day in a pillar of cloud, to lead them the way; and by night in a pillar of fire, to give them light; to go by day and night. His people will bless him all day long. Bless us with abundant crops and prosperous businesses throughout the land, even on the mountains, plains, and valley; Let there be fruit like that of no other nations in our land; may the cities be as full of people as the fields are of grass. We speak to our leader and say thus saith the Lord, therefore now go, lead the people unto the place of which I have spoken unto you: behold, mine angel shall go before you: nevertheless in the day when I visit I will visit their sin upon them. His name will be honored forever; it will continue as the sun; and all will be blessed in him; all nations will praise him. Blessed be Jehovah God, the God of America, who only does wonderful things. Blessed be his glorious name forever. Let the whole earth be filled with his glory. Lord, lead our president, and cause him to set no strange gods before him or trust in the arm of flesh. Lead the president, O Lord, in thy righteousness, because of our enemies; make the way of our leader straight before your face. Lead him in thy truth, and teach him your ways, for you are the God of his salvation. Our president will wait upon God all day long. Teach our leaders your ways of obedience. Let them understand that obedience is better than sacrifice and that the wages of sin is death. Lead the president in a plain path and destroy his enemies. For the Lord is a rock and a fortress to our leader; therefore for God's name sake, lead our president and guide him. O send out thy light and thy truth: let them lead our president; let them bring him unto your holy hill, and to your tabernacles. Lord bring our leader out of blindness by a way that he knows not; and lead him in paths that he has not known: make darkness light before him, and crooked paths straight. These things will God do for our leader, and not forsake him.

WISDOM TO LEAD

God, it is written in your word that you are no respecter of person. Therefore, I ask you in the name of Jesus Christ to appear unto me in dreams and speak with me in my understanding. Give me an understanding heart to judge your people, that I may discern good from bad. I believe that the things I pray and ask for in prayer I receive them according to your words. Behold, God has done according to his words. He has given me a wise and understanding heart; so there was none like me before or after shall any arise like me. God has also given me that which I have not asked for, both riches and honor and length of days. God quicken my mortal body with the spirit of wisdom, knowledge and understanding in Jesus name. Lord, I thank you for blessing me with the power of wisdom, knowledge and understanding. Lord, I ask in the name of Jesus that you bless me with the spirit of power and might. Lord, I thank you for giving me your precious spirit of power and might for your glory and honor in Jesus name, that my joy may be full. Lord, I thank you that you have given unto me to know the mysteries of your kingdom for nothing is secret, that shall not be made manifest unto me neither anything hid that shall not be made known and come to light. Wisdom is justified of all her children and is more precious than silver and gold. I hold fast to wisdom and get understanding and apply the knowledge of God to all that I do. The wisdom of God is written upon my heart and I will not depart from the knowledge of God. Keep your words before my eyes and cause me not to wonder from your pathway of life and godliness all the days of my life.

A NEW BEGINNING

God, I thank you for keeping me focus on the mark of preaching the gospel everywhere I go, in season and out of season. My goal is to preach, teach, heal and deliver with signs and wonders following. Lord, I thank you for bringing me and my family back home at the appointed time. Thank you for blessing those who bless us and those who curse us. God, send me anointed, Holy Ghost filled mentors to help me to accomplish my task, you have purposed for me in Jesus name. Provide for all the needs of my ministry and keep me pure and holy before you and men. God, thank you for marriage and family in due season and I declare no delays in Jesus name. Cause my glory to be great and remembered in you. Lord, deliver me from treacherous people and give me a new, clean, pure heart to love people. Remove the hurt, the pain, the rejection, the bitterness, the anger and the deception from me concerning my friends and enemies. Release me from any individual who abandons and deserts me. Free me to move into the realm of the supernatural spirit of God. Give me the wisdom of God and the faith of God to believe nothing is impossible and to do the impossible according to the word of God. Make me great in Jesus. Cause me to rise above my enemies and let no evil befalls me. Give me rain in dry season and wheat in drought. Provide for me all that I have need of and give me more than enough. Always bless my friends and my enemies. Cause my seed to be mighty and great upon the earth. Send warring angels ahead of me and on every assignment and surround me with a shield of glory, fire, water and the blood of Jesus

Christ. Make my name to be remembered over all the earth. Bring Judgment Lord and show your power and manifest your glory everywhere I go to preach and minister. I call for your manifested presence as in the days of the tabernacle; with the Ark of the Covenant. Lord, let me be the ark that carries your glory to the people. Lord, let this vessel contain your glory with miracles, upon top of miracles of miracles in Jesus name. Bestow to me the gifts you bestowed upon Jesus and the greater works. My Lord, cause me to see through the eyes of God. Give me the mind of Christ and cause me to speak oracles with the spirit of God. Cause my foundation to be strong, pure, sanctified and established according to the principles of God. Prepare me for war and use me in battle and give me victory every moment of my life in Jesus name. Amen.

THE LORD'S GUIDANCE

The Lord will guide me continually, and satisfy my needs in parched places, and make my bones strong; and I shall be like a watered garden. My ancient ruins shall be rebuilt; I shall raise up the foundation of many generations; I shall be called the repairer of the breach, the restorer of streets to live in. Build up, build up, prepare the way, and remove every obstruction from God's people's way. I will prepare the way of the Lord. I will make his paths straight. I will call God's peoples to repentance. I will tell them Jesus is coming soon and cause them to turn from their sins and iniquity before it is too late. For Jesus will come suddenly like a thief in the night without warning and many will be left behind in amazement and disbelief of His sudden visitation. I take delight in the Lord, and He makes me ride upon the heights of the earth; God will feed me with the heritage of my ancestor Jacob. My iniquities have been barriers between me and my God. I have prepared the way for the people, I build up, and I build the highway and clear it of stones. They have chosen their own ways and their souls delight in their abominations; God also will choose harsh treatment for them and will bring upon them what they dread. For when God called, no one answered, when God spoke, no one listened. They did evil in God's sight and chose what displeased Him. God will extend peace to me like a river, and the wealth of nations like a flooding stream. As a mother comforts her child, so will God comfort me. The hand of the Lord will be made known to me. And God, because of their actions and their imaginations is about to come and gather all nations and tongues, and they will come and see God's glory. All mankind will come and bow down before God, says the Lord. And they will go out and look upon the dead bodies of those who rebelled against God. God has sent an angel before me to prepare the way. God has sent my angel before me to make straight the crooked path. The angel of the Lord has gone before me to bring me into God's promise. God has made my way perfect for his glory and honor. God send me your Glory to take me into your promise. Teach me your ways Lord and give me your presence and show me your glory. Go with me and before me Lord that I will know you are with me and have chosen me for this task. Keep me in all of your ways so that I will never fail. Show me favor and give me rest because you said you have given me rest and favor with man and God. Let everyone know you are pleased with me and know me by name. Show me your power and show me your face. God will go with me everywhere I go because he promised to lead and guide me into his promises. God, speak to me face to face and mouth to mouth. Teach me your ways and keep me in your presence. God, do the very things I ask you to do. God, magnify yourself in every area of my life. Take me into the land of promise. Drive out my enemies from before me. Let me inquire of you Lord and let your cloud of glory be the sign that you are with me. Do not send me anywhere God, without your presence and your power. Show me your face God and show me your glory. God, take me up into the land flowing with milk and honey. Bless me Lord and make my name great. God, teach me your ways so I may know you. What will distinguish me from the rest of the people in all the earth. God knows me by name and has shown me favor. God will do what I ask. God have mercy and compassion upon me. God will go with me every where I go. Amen.

<u>RESTORATION</u>

For it is written, God will restore me the years that the locust, the cankerworm, the caterpillar and the palmerworm has eaten. Thus Lord, I thank you for restoring my entire life back unto me in Jesus name. Everything that I have lost, given up, had stolen from me and delayed restore now O Mighty God of Israel in Jesus name. Restore my home, finance, family, business, ministry, health, deliverance, healing, power, faith, hope, joy, happiness, trust, love, success, prosperity, and stability. Bless me Lord beyond my wildest dreams. Make my darkness light and cause me to see your handy work in my life and glorify you in heaven. Restore me to the powers of Adam and the promises of Jesus Christ to do what he has done and the greater works. Restore peace, mercy and forgiveness unto me in Jesus name. Make me great and my name famous above the earth for your namesake. Let me be a joy unto you Lord and always pleasing you. Restore me in every area that I am weak or torn down. Restore my anointing, restore my unwavering faith and trust in you God. Restore the Gifts to heal sickness and disease. Restore the anointing to cast out demons and evil spirit in Jesus name. Restore the hedge of protection and the anointing on my life. Let righteousness and humility be my covering unto you Lord. Keep me true, pure and holy all the days of my life. Let no destruction befall me or any evil come near me. Cause me to see your clear pathway and your perfect will for my life daily in Jesus name. Restore my body with rest when I am tired and weary and have given out of my virtue, pour yourself back into me in Jesus name. Give me wisdom of great insight and make me of a quick study in Jesus name. Restore my finance and my ministry. Restore my children, home and businesses and cause me to prosper and to be blessed to be a blessing to others. Restore my family. Save my parent's entire household and use my family gloriously in the works of the ministry, bless and prosper my family with miracles, signs and wonders following them. Cover my entire family in the blood of Jesus Christ and let no evil befalls my family nor let any evil come near their dwelling that would harm them in Jesus name. Make all unbelievers in my family believers.

THE POWER OF THE HOLY SPIRIT

The spirit that is upon you and my words that I have put in your mouth shall not depart out of your mouth. Nations shall come to your light. They come to you. The abundance of the sea shall be brought to you. The wealth of the nations shall come to you. They shall bring gold. They shall bring their silver and gold to honor the Lord because, He has glorified you. Foreigners shall build up your walls and their kings shall minister to you. Your gates shall always be open; so that nations shall bring you their wealth. For the nation and kingdom that will not serve you shall perish. The descendants of those who oppressed you shall come bending low to you, and all who despised you shall bow down at your feet. I will make you majestic forever, a joy from age to age. You will suck the milk of the nations. You shall suck the breasts of kings. I will appoint peace as your overseer and righteousness as your taskmaster. You shall call your walls salvation and your gates praise. Your God will be your glory. Your people shall all be righteous. They shall posses the land forever. Strangers shall stand and feed your flocks; foreigners shall till your land and dress your vines. You shall be called priest of the Lord, you shall be named ministers of our God. You shall enjoy the wealth of the nations. They shall posses a double portion. He has clothed me with the garments of salvation. He has covered me with the robe of righteousness. The nations shall see your vindication and you shall be called by a new name that the mouth of God shall give. You shall be a crown of beauty in the hand of the Lord and a royal diadem in the hand of your God. You shall be no more be termed forsaken for your land shall be married. Say to the daughter of Zion, see your salvation comes and you shall be sought out a city not forsaken. No more shall there be in it an infant that lives but a few days or an old person who does not live out a lifetime. My chosen shall long enjoy the work of their hands. Before they call I will answer and while they are speaking I will hear. Amen.

THE ANOINTING OF GOD

In the name of Jesus I raise the dead, heal the sick, and speak in new tongues, cast out demons and evil spirits. I walk in miracles with signs and wonders following the words I speak. I am the ark of God's covenant carrying his glory to the nations. The fear of God is upon me. No evil will befall me no harm will overtake me and no evil will come near my dwelling place. I have the power to speak life and death. I have defeated Satan, he is under my feet. I have pursued my enemies and overtaken, spoiled them and recovered all. God has restored me all. The witches and the workers of iniquity are consumed with fire from heaven in my presence. God has removed all evil workers of witchcraft and iniquity workers far from me. Hell trembles with fear at the thought of me. Demons flee before me in fear. I expose the kingdom of darkness with my light of holiness, righteousness, sanctification and purification. I am a money magnet. Money, wealth, riches and prosperity is overtaking me. All my needs are met. I walk in divine health. I walk in the perfect will of God for my life. I am without spot, wrinkle or blemish. God has given me the heathen for my inheritance. I have the favor of God and man. The windows of heaven are opened unto me and God is pouring out blessings upon me more than I have room enough to receive. I have no lack. I am blessed to be a blessing. I am a gift from God. I am a woman of virtue and honor. I have supernatural wisdom and the supernatural revelations of God. I speak with the voice of an oracle. I am God's mouth piece. I am a prayer warrior. I have the tongue of a warrior. God's name is written upon my forehead for all to see. I have the gift of discernments. I am anointed to go places and walk through closed doors. I am a lender and not a borrower. I am a giver and a receiver. I am the head and not the tail. I am going over and not under. I am above and not beneath. I have the anointing and the power to decree and declare the words of God and see it's instant miraculous manifestations. I am bold and fearless. I am humble and patient. I am a world changer and a world traveler. I am great, famous and successful. Satan is under my feet, and I have defeated all my enemies for they are no more. I win, I win, and I win. I have the power, the anointing and the glory of God to do the greater works. I have launch out into the deep and have entered a new dimension in the spirit realm. Because they that know their God shall do exploit in the deep. I am in total agreement with God and whatsoever God says it is so. I have been transformed into an instrument of God for his glory. Nothing is impossible unto me. I believe in the word of God. I believe I will do the greater works. I believe I will do exploits. I believe what I ask God for in the name of Jesus Christ, He will do, because God cannot lie. I believe that God will establish a people that knows him and calls upon his name.

GOD'S POWER TO MAN

God has given me power over unclean spirits. I have power to heal sickness and to cast out devils. All power is given unto me in heaven and earth. I sit at the right hand of God and bless his holy name. I have power to forgive sin. Jesus has given me power from heaven and in the earth against unclean spirits, to cast them out and to heal all manner of sickness and disease. The kingdom of God has power. I am walking in the spirit and the power of God. The Holy Ghost has come upon me and the power of the highest has overshadowed me. I return to the nations in the power of the spirit of God and my fame has been made known all over the earth. When I speak, my words are with power that produces results and astonishment. I have authority and power, thus I command unclean spirits to come out and they obey me. The power of the Lord is always present in my life to heal the people of all their sickness and diseases. God has given me power and authority over all devils and to cure all disease. Everyone who sees me is all amazed at the mighty powers of God in my life. Jesus has given me power to thread on serpents and scorpions and over all the powers of the enemy and nothing shall by any means hurt me and no evil shall befall me. Through mighty signs and wonders, by the power of the spirit of God I am preaching the gospel of Jesus Christ. I have power to establish myself according to the word of God. My preaching is with demonstration of the Spirit and of the power of God. My faith is standing in the power of God. The anointing and the power of Jesus Christ rest upon me in Jesus name. Amen.

PRAYER FOR MINISTRY

I grew and waxed strong in spirit, filled with wisdom and the grace of God was upon me. I increased in wisdom and stature and in favor with God and man. The spirit of the Lord is upon me. For God has anointed me to preach the gospel to the poor. He has sent me to heal the broken hearted, to preach deliverance to the captives and, recovering of sight to the blind, He has sent me to set at liberty them that are bruised and to preach the acceptable year of the Lord. My faith has saved me. Whosoever receives me in the name of the Lord receives Jesus Christ. God shall avenge me his own elect speedily when I cry unto him. God will give me help and deliverance from my enemies when I cry unto Him day and night. Lord, not my will, but your will be done in my life. Father, into your hands have I committed my spirit. Lord, open my understanding that I will understand the scriptures. I shall see heaven opened up and the angels of the Lord ascending and descending upon the earth all the days of my life. I know the voice of God and will follow his voice but the voice of a stranger I will not follow and will flee from the voice of a stranger. I live in Christ and Christ lives in me. I produce much fruit in the spirit because God's word lives in my heart. Whatsoever I ask of the father in Jesus name, I will receive if I doubt not in my heart when I pray and ask. Before God formed me in the belly, God knew me and before I was born God sanctified me and ordained me a prophet unto the nations. The Lord is my light and my salvation. The Lord is my strength. The Lord is my shepherd. I shall not want of any good thing. Discretion shall preserve me and understanding shall keep me. I shall find favor and good understanding in the sight of God and man. I trust in the Lord with all my heart. I will not depend on my own understanding but I will depend on the Lords. I fear the Lord and depart form evil. I honor the Lord with all my substance and he has blessed me with plenty. Blessings are upon my head. I will receive the desires of my heart. I am taught of the Lord and great is my peace. I shall be established in righteousness. I shall be far from oppression; for I shall not fear and far from terror; for it shall not come near me. Whosoever shall gather together against me shall fall. No weapons that are formed against me shall prosper; and every tongue that shall rise against me in judgment I condemn now in Jesus name. Amen.

SIGNS, WONDERS AND MIRACLES

Lord, I thank you for sending me forth into all the nations to preach the gospel. I thank you for working with me and confirming your words with signs following. I thank you for the multitude that believe in you, and is saved, baptized in water and in the Holy Spirit and have eternal life. In the name of Jesus I cast out devils; speak in new tongues, raise the dead, lay hands on the sick and they recover. For with God nothing shall be impossible. Because I believe on the Lord, the work that Jesus Christ has done, I will do also and greater works. And whatsoever I ask in Jesus name he will do, that the father may be glorified in the son. If I ask anything in Jesus name, Jesus will do it. Now father; in the name of Jesus glorify me with your own self with the glory that I had with thee before the world was. Holy Spirit, breathe on me that I will receive you in the fullness and magnitude of your awesome power. God, in my ministry pour out your spirit upon all flesh and cause our sons and daughters to prophecy and show your wonders in heaven above and signs in the earth beneath, blood and fire and vapor of smoke. Cause the praises of God to rise above the heavens and give me favor with all people and add to the churches daily by my hands. Lord, let there be many signs and wonders manifest themselves in the midst of the people. Let the sick be brought out into the streets and laid on beds and couches, that at the least my shadow shall pass over them and they shall all be healed in Jesus name. God, give me the power and spirit to obey you always rather than man at all cost. Anoint me God with the Holy Ghost and with power, I go to do good and heal all that are oppressed of the devil for God is with me. Lord, grant me the desires of my heart to perform signs and wonders by my hands for your glory in Jesus name. Lord let the multitude declare the miracles and wonders God has wrought by my hands in the midst of the people. Let the sinners be drawn to you seeking salvation saying what must I do to be saved in Jesus name. God, in the name of Jesus, I ask you for household salvation for every sinner that is saved in our ministry. Let the word of God that I speak proceed out of my mouth like sharp swords and piercing arrows to the hearts of men to bring total submission and yielding to the Holy Spirit of the living God in Jesus name. Let a cloud of glory hover over every ministry I operate in. Lead me and guide me by your Holy Spirit in Jesus name all the days of my life. For I know that, whatsoever God doeth, it shall be for ever: nothing can be put to it, nor any thing taken from it: and God doeth it, that men should fear before him. I will not be conformed to this world: but I will be transformed by the renewing of my mind, that I may prove the good, acceptable, and perfect, will of God. God, you have made me a sign unto the people and the nations. Thus, I declare your marvelous and wonderful miracles in the midst of the people. Amen.

THE LORD'S HANDMAIDEN

For the Lord will be unto me and this nation a wall of fire round about and will be the glory in the midst of me and this nation. The Lord has spread me abroad as the four winds of the heaven. After the glory hath the Lord sent me unto the nations which spoiled me. For anyone or anything that touch me touch the apple of God's eye. For behold, God will shake his hand upon them, and they shall be a spoil to their servants and you shall know that God has sent me. Sing and rejoice, O daughter of mine for I have come unto thee and will dwell in the midst of thee, and the nations will know that the Lord of host has favored me and sent me to them. Be silent, O all flesh, before the Lord for he is raised up out of his holy habitation. Satan, the Lord rebuked you O Satan; even the Lord that hath chosen this nation rebukes you. Is not this a brand plucked out of the fire? Behold my child I have caused your iniquity to pass from you, and I will clothe you with change of raiment. If thou will walk in my ways, and if thou will keep my charge, then you shall also judge my house, and shall also keep my courts, and I will give thee places to walk among these that stand by. My daughter, you will accomplish everything I placed in your heart to do, not by might, nor by power but by my spirit, saith the Lord of host. Who art thou, O great mountain? Before my handmaiden, thou shall become a plain; and she shall bring forth the headstone thereof with shouting, crying, grace, grace unto it. The hand of the Lord's handmaid has laid the foundation of this house, her hands shall also finish it; and thou shalt know that the Lord of host hath sent me unto you. Because she did not despise her small beginnings the Lord has blessed her and made her great. Amen.

FATHERS AND DADS

God, I thank you for my father. You have blessed him with salvation, strength and deliverance. The gates of hell will not prevail against him. You have made him the head and not the tail. He is going over and not under. He is rich and prospering in the things of God. He is laying treasures up in heaven and he has laid treasures upon the earth as inheritance for his children and his children's children. No weapons formed against him will prosper. You have made him stronger than all his enemies and given him power and authority over his household. We are obedient to him. We honor and respect him. We stand beside and behind him to strengthen his arm in battles. He protects and provides an abundant supply of all that we need. His love for his family is revealed in his concern, his tenderness and his faithfulness towards his household. My dad is a righteous man who loves and obeys the Lord, God Almighty. He lays his hand upon our heads and decrees the blessings of the Lord upon our lives. He walks in the realm of the supernatural faith and miracles of God. Like Adam and Enoch he walks with God daily. Like Noah and Jeremiah he obeys God even at the point of mocking. Like Abraham and Jacob, my dad is a friend of God. Like Isaac and Jesus so is my dad the child of promise. Like Joseph and Moses so is my dad a leader. Like Joshua and Gideon so is my father a mighty warrior of God. Like David and Daniel so is my father a man after God's own heart. Like Elijah so is my father a servant of the Lord. Like Samuel and Ezekiel so is my father a prophet of the Lord. Like Solomon, so is my dad the wisest man of God. He fears the Lord. He walks not by sight but by faith. He is not moved nor is he troubled by the storms of life because he calls those things that are not as thou they were and they became what he calls forth in the name of Jesus. My father is created in the image and likeness of God, a little lower than God. My father is a king and is of a royal priesthood and his words have power. He has the power of life and death in his tongue and he chooses to speak life in every situation. My father is a mighty man of God and knows no limit with God. He takes God at his word; therefore nothing is impossible for him. He thinks in his heart the desires of God and he becomes the desires of God. My father is the high priest of our home and he leads us before the throne of God with praise and thanksgiving in our mouth. The words my father speaks are sharper than a two-edge sword, because God has crafted his tongue and placed a sword in his mouth to do justice. My father is healed from the crown of his head to the soul of his feet and shall never know sickness. God has established my father in the high places, high above the gates of the elders where his fame has spread upon the face of the earth. All hell trembles at the presence and the voice of my father because he is the anointed son of God. Jesus is Lord of my father's life. The word of God is written upon my father's heart and he will not sin against God. I claim every blessing and every promise that God made Abraham for my father in the name of Jesus Christ. My daddy belongs to God and God watches over him day and night. No evil shall befall my daddy and great is his peace. My daddy loves God and God loves my daddy. I thank God for loosing all my father's angels to perfect everything that concerns him daily. Make his way straight before him and remove every obstacle from his path in Jesus name.

MOTHERS AND MOMS

Dear God, precious Jesus and Holy Spirit, thank you for my mother. I call my mother saved filled with the Holy Spirit and operating in the gifts of the spirit with the evidence of speaking in tongues. She is blessed of the Lord God Almighty and cannot be cursed. No weapons formed against her shall prosper. Every tongue of judgment and lies that rises up against her, I condemn in the name of Jesus Christ. Her children calls her blessed and is blessing her daily. She lacks nothing for God is her provider that meets all her needs in abundance. Her friends' calls her blessed and is blessing her. Her enemies' calls her blessed and is blessing her. She rises up from the ground of humility like a mighty giant ready to do battle for the glory of the Lord. Her houses are blessed and God continues to add more houses unto her supernaturally. She is prospering in every good works and her finances are growing in leaps and bounds because she gives unto the Lord freely and cheerfully. Her business is expanding and producing great financial increase because El Shaddai has opened the windows of heaven and poured out blessings upon her. Her children are blessed and are highly favored upon the face of the earth. Her grandchildren are blessed and are prospering in the works of the Lord. Her great grandchildren's ways have been made perfect before the Lord God Almighty. She is surrounded by host of angels assigned to bring her into all the promises of God for her life. Her strength is renewed daily and her youth is renewed like an eagle. She will live a long, healthy and prosperous life. She will never be alone all the days of her life. The mate that God has given her has been restored unto her without delay. Her ways before God has been made clear and straight. God has put his spirit in her and has revealed his secrets and mysteries unto her. She has produced a great nation for the glory of God. She sets nothing ungodly before her eyes. She speaks no guile or evil with her tongue. She is bold in the Lord. The spirit of love has enveloped her and has over flown her banks. She has made peace her hiding place and joy her house of defense. She is rich and abounds with blessings for the Lord has crowned her with his glory. She has no want or lack of any good thing. She is abundantly blessed. She is a lender unto many and not a borrower. All her bills are paid in full. She enjoys life to the fullest. She embraces every day with gratitude. She loves her children and grandchildren and lifts them high before God daily. My mother enjoys the fruits of her labor and her work for God is not in vain. She walks before God holy and pure in spirit and in truth. I call my mother a mighty woman of God who prophetically intercedes for her family daily. She does not hold her peace but she stands on the walls of defense and make mention of our names before God daily. She is a travailing woman of God that cries before God for the needs of her family to be met. She is a virtuous woman and there is none like her. My mother is most valuable and precious to her family. Her ways are unto God and her will are unto God. Her desires are unto the Lord and her heart belongs only to the Lord. She runs to and fro upon the earth like a mighty giant destroying every work of the devil sent against her family. She is a mother that does not give up on her children but hope against hopelessness. She has the gift of faith, healing and miracles in Jesus name. My mother is a queen established in the righteousness of God for all generation. The words my mother speaks are good and full of life. The Lord has made my mother a defended city this day. My mother has extended life because she has found favor with God. My mother health returns to her quickly. The favor of God has caused my mother to have great financial blessings upon her life. People are amazed at how the Lord has blessed my mother. My mother secures her possession in the fear of the Lord. Amen.

CHILD AND CHILDREN

(Child's name) grew and waxed strong in spirit, filled with wisdom. The grace of God was upon him. (Child's name) increased in wisdom and stature and in favor with God and man. The spirit of the Lord is

71

upon him; because, God has anointed (Child's name) to preach the gospel to the poor. He hath sent him to heal the brokenhearted, to preach deliverance to the captives and recovering of sight to the blind, to set at liberty them that are bound and to declare the acceptable year of the Lord. (Child's name) faith has saved him. Whosoever shall receive (Child's name) in the name of the Lord receiveth Jesus Christ. God shall avenge (Child's name) His own elect speedily, which cry day and night unto him. Lord, let your will be done in (Child's name) life. Father into your hands I have commend (Child's name) spirit. The Lord opened (Child's name) understanding that he might understand the scriptures. I shall see heaven open and the angels of God ascending and descending upon him. (Child's name) knows the voice of God and follows God's voice and flees from the voice of a stranger. He abides in Christ and Christ abides in him and he bears much fruit. God's words abide in (Child's name) heart and whatsoever (Child's name) ask of the father in Jesus name he receiveth. Before God formed (Child's name) in the belly, God knew him and before he was birth out of my womb, God sanctified him and ordained him a prophet unto the nations. The Lord is the light and salvation of (Child's name). The Lord is his strength. The Lord is his shepherd; he shall not want. Discretion shall preserve (Child's name) and understanding shall keep him. The fear of the Lord is upon him and God's way is made clear before him. In righteousness shall (Child's name) be established. He receives the desires of his heart and no weapons that are formed against him shall prosper, for God has made him fair by the multitude of his branches; so that all the trees of The

Garden of Eden, that were in the garden of God, envied (Child's name). He is a precious gift from God to me and his father and the seed of righteousness whose blessings are of the Lord, God Almighty. (Child's name) shall be established according to the will, plan and purpose of God without delays or obstacles in Jesus name. Amen.

DECEPTION AND ERROR

Father, prevent my children from being deceived or walk contrary to the will of God for their lives. Keep my children faithful unto death that they may stand before God a worthy and holy vessel of honor and glory unto God all the days of their lives.

WHAT OUR CHILDREN LISTEN

Lord, let the music my children listen to brings you glory and honor. Let them passionately hate and detest secular music. Let praise and worship music be the center of their lives. Let them sing unto you Lord in the beauty of holiness.

WHAT OUR CHILDREN WATCH

Lord let my children set no evil before their sight. Let my children reject and detest every sexually perverted material. Let my children not desire or set their sights upon filthy pornographic media or materials. Let not my children look upon anyone or anything with lust of the eye or lust of the flesh. Give my children a way of escape and cause them to take it for all temptation that would cause them to sin and defile the temple of the living God. Separate my children from peers with ungodly lust and desires for perversion and keep my children protected from wolf in sheep's clothing in Jesus name.

COUNSEL FOR OUR CHILDREN

Let the advice of my children's ungodly friends become foolishness unto them. Let my children not walk in the council of the ungodly or sit in the seat of the scornful. Let my children be delivered from evil men with perverted hearts and ways of homosexual desires. Protect my children from every evil powers, forces, principalities and rulers of darkness. Lord preserve my children from all evil and preserve the souls of my children from death and destruction all the days of their lives.

BLESSINGS AND PROTECTION FOR CHILDREN & FRIENDS

Heavenly Father, bless my children and their friends in every area of their lives. Keep my children and their friends from ungodly counsel and corrupt morals and reprobate mindset. Father, keep my children and their friends from bad companies and bad places and bad things. Keep them safe from all harm and danger in Jesus name. Heavenly Father, protect my children and their friends in the world and hide your words in their hearts that they will not sin against you O Lord. Put the fear of God in my children and their friend's heart and cause them to reverence God and not use the Lord's name in vain. God give my children lasting friendship with peers after your own heart, purpose and will. Lead my children down the path of righteousness, holiness and sanctification. Let everything my children does glorify you in Jesus name. Lead my children and their friends done the path of truth, righteousness, health, prosperity and favor. Open doors of opportunity in their lives where you want them to go and close door for wrong opportunities in their lives where you do not want them to go in Jesus name.

CHILDREN'S PROTECTION FROM ENEMY

Keep my children safe from the snares which their enemies have setup for them and the gins of the workers of iniquity. Let the wicked fall into their own nets while my children escapes unharmed. Let my children's enemies fall into their own traps which they have set up for my children in Jesus name. Show and give my children a way of escape in every situation that does not glorify you Mighty God all the days of their lives.

JOURNEY AND TRAVELING

Father, God I speak traveling mercy over my children as they travel throughout the land all the days of their lives. I bind and reject all accidents from my children in Jesus name. I bid my children God speed in all their journey and decree and declare no harm will come to my children and no evil will befall my children all the days of their lives. Their ways have been made clear and straight before them for God have given his angels charge over them to keep them in all their ways. No sickness or disease will attack my children's body, mind or spirit as they travel near and far daily. Their lives and pathways will be easy because I have sent the word of God before them to establish all their ways before the Lord. All my children's needs are met and they have abundance in all things. My children have chosen to walk in the pathway of righteousness all the days of their lives.

PRODIGAL AND REBELLIOUS CHILDREN

My prodigal child will return in humility. Now God keep this child safe and protected from all harm and danger and let no evil powers have dominion over my prodigal child who is in rebellion against me and you. Heavenly Father, I ask in the name of Jesus that you bring my prodigal child home quickly and safely unto me and cause this child to recover all out of the snare of the devil. God, reconcile this child back unto you.

GOD'S KINGDOM IN YOUR CHILD

God, establish your kingdom in my children and cause them to walk as your high priest in righteousness, of the Most High God all the days of their lives. Cause my children to have godly fame in the gates of the elders that men may see their good works and glorify you. Let their words and actions never bring a reproach to the name of God. Let your kingdom come in my children's lives and let your will be done in them. Order their foot steps in your word and cause them to follow Jesus Christ all the days of their life. God, you have made a vow unto me concerning my children, forget not your promise to me and establish my children as promised.

MY DAUGHTER

My daughter is mighty upon the face of the earth. She is beautiful, fearfully and wonderfully made in the image of God. She is a woman of virtue hidden in the heart of God. My daughter has been crafted in the hands of God and molded into perfection. She hopes in glory and her faith and trust is in God. She is the king's daughter, dressed in royal garments trimmed with purple and gold. She is greatly admired and blessed of the Lord. My daughter is peculiar and of a royal priesthood. She is the daughter of Zion, erected in the house of God as a tower of light. She is the warrior of God, leaping over walls and running upon her enemies like mighty giants. She is God's battle-axe, sword of judgment, rod of correction and sharp threshing instruments. No weapons formed against her shall prosper; they shall all fail to destroy her. No enemies that rise against her shall prevail against her. My daughter is the head only and not the tail. She is above and not beneath. She is rich and walking in prosperity. She is healed and walks in divine healing. She lives in abundance and lacks nothing. The daughters of the world envy her and bring her gifts. The wealth of the wicked is given to her. Blessings are overtaking her. The windows of heaven are opened unto her and pouring out blessings upon her more than she has room to receive. My daughter is fearless and matchless in battle. She is Sarah's daughter and the child of promise. She is the bride of Christ ready for his return. My daughter is flawless and unmovable in all her ways unto God. God has lifted her up in the high places to declare his words. She has been bought with the blood of Jesus Christ and the life she lives is

not her own but Jesus Christ. She is a praise and
worship instrument of God. She enters into his gates
with thanksgiving in her mouth. The angels of the
Lord encampeth around her and no evil shall befall
her. Great is her peace. Her husband calls her blessed
and her children calls her blessed, for the Lord has
blessed her and made her name great upon the earth.
My daughter is blessed to be a blessing to others. She
speaks with the voice of oracles and great men and
women seek her out for counsel. My daughter is a
trader and commerce with merchants of nations.
Much has been given unto her and much is required
of her. She is the handmaiden of the Lord, clothe
with humility and patience. My daughter travails and
wails for the promises of God. She is unstoppable
and her line of defense is secure. The word of God is
written upon her heart that she will not sin against
God. God's word is her shield of defense and coat of
armor. Jesus is Lord over my daughter's life and she
stand on the word of God's promise and prophecy
for her life. God will give my daughter the desires of
her heart and bring every promise He made unto her
come to pass in her life. My daughter will have a long
and healthy life. My daughter is heaven bound and
will reign with Jesus Christ. Her name is written in the
book of life and her name is known in the kingdom
of darkness and hell trembles at the sound and sight
of her. Her voice shall be heard in all the nations.
Nothing shall be impossible unto my daughter
because she believes in Jesus Christ. The spirit of the
Lord has anointed my daughter to walk into the realm
of the supernatural with signs and wonders following
her. Her gifts will make room for her and bring her
before great men. The favor of the Lord is upon her.

The words that she speaks have life and are powerful and accomplish what she sent them out to do. God has given her grace and His mercy is sufficient for her in Jesus name. Amen.

MY SON

Lord, thank you for my son the prophet and the priest, in whom I am well pleased. Crown him with wisdom, knowledge and understanding and use him for your glory. God, I thank you for giving me a son in your image and likeness. Lord send an angel before my son to prosper his ways. God, bless my son as you have blessed Isaac, the son of Abraham. Lord, bring good success and favor to my son. Lord, let people serve him and let nations bow down before him. Bless those who bless him and curse those who curse him. Let him rule over many nations. God, place a coat of many colors upon my son as a sign of your favor towards him. My son is a prophet that shall save his people. People are amazed at the miracles that are demonstrated by the hand of my son. Lord have mercy on my son. Make him a wise and faithful servant to rule over your house and give him meat in due season. Clothe him in righteousness and feed him your word. Give him the gifts of the spirit and cause him to do exploit in your name O Lord. My son is the salt of the earth and the light of the world. My son speaks with gracious words and all wonder at his intellect. My son is wise and wins souls for the Lord. This is the last days and God has poured out his spirit upon my son and he is prophesying. The blessings of Abraham are on my son. My son rejoices in his heart for the opportunity to enter the house of God with blessings and praises. God has blessed my son with all spiritual blessings in heavenly places with Christ Jesus. God will bless my son and multiply him as the stars of the sky and the sand of the sea. My son eyes are blessed for they see and his ears blessed for they hear. My son shall inherit the kingdom of God. Blessed is he who is not offended in my son. The grace of God is upon my son all the days of his life and the peace of God shall be his pavilion in Jesus name. Amen.

REPENTING HEART OF A SON

Heavenly, Father give my son a repenting heart when he sins. Cause my child to seek the kingdom of God first and all His righteousness and then add everything he has need of unto him in abundance. Father, let there be no lack in my son's life and give him no room for spoil. Break every chain that binds him and cause him to flee from captivity through his praise and worship. Contend, O Lord, with those who contend with my son, fight against those who fight against him. Take up shield and buckler, arise and come to my son's aid when he is in trouble. My son will serve the Lord all the days of his life. Bless him with the favor of God and man and excels him in everything he does. If my son confesses his sins, God I know you are faithful and just to forgive him of his sins and purify him from all unrighteousness. Therefore, I thank you for giving my son a repenting heart. My son loves the Lord, God with his whole heart and sets up no idols in his heart. My son ways has not caused him to stray from the path that the Lord has established for him all the days of his life. My son is blessed with the wisdom of God. Amen.

SON'S FUTURE WIFE

Prepare my son's wife for him and prepare my son for his wife, even now that when they meet they will both know and confirm that they are the right ones for each other. My son's future wife will be a virtuous woman filled with the Spirit of God and walking in the anointing of God. Let them be married until death do they part. Let nothing or no one hinder or separate their relationship and matrimonial union together. Let them be exclusively for each other only. Let his future wife not be touched by another man nor let him touch another woman except each other after they are married. Close and seal every door of lust and temptation unto them and prevent them from going astray from each other or have spoil for another. Bring them together at the appointed time, while they are still young. Protect them from strange men and women and keep them free from perversion in Jesus name. Amen.

DAUGHTER'S FUTURE HUSBAND

Prepare my daughter's husband for her and prepare my daughter for her husband, even now that when they meet they will both know and confirm that they are the right ones for each other. Let them be married until death do they part. Let nothing or no one hinder or separate their relationship and matrimonial union together. Let them be exclusively for each other only. Let her future husband not be touched by another woman nor let him touch another woman except each other after they are married. Close and seal every door of lust and temptation unto them and prevent them from going astray from each other or have spoiled for another. Bring them together at the appointed time, while they are still young. Send my daughter's husband in search for her and when he finds her let him know that she is the wife you have prepared for him before they were born. Her future husband will be a man of honor, integrity and compassion. He will have a passion for God like David. He will prophecy with accuracy like Samuel. He will be full of wisdom like Solomon. He will be a leader like Moses. But most importantly he will be a friend of God like Abraham. He will be like his big brother Jesus. He shall be a mighty man of valor and shall be known in the gates of the elders. Protect them from strange men and women and keep them free from perversion in Jesus name. Amen.

DESIRES OF THE HEART FOR FAMILY

Thank you Lord for my entire family's salvation; because, it is written, believe in the Lord and you and your whole household shall be saved. I thank you for mother's spiritual conversion. Fill mother with the Holy Spirit with the evidence of speaking in tongues. Make her into a mighty woman of God. I call mother a mighty prophetess and a great intercessor. Guide her Holy Spirit by the way she should go. Remove perversion and foul speaking from her mouth. Lord clean her mouth with hot coals of fire and wash her with hyssop. Purge mother and make her clean. Put righteousness, holiness and sanctification upon her all the days of her life. Clothe my mother in your glory Lord and watch over her all the days of her life. Lord, I thank you for my father's salvation. Cause my father to freely walk into your precious light of wisdom, knowledge and understanding. Make his crooked paths straight before him that he will serve you all the days of his life in spirit and in truth. Baptize my father with water and with Holy Ghost fire. Make my father a mighty man of valor and spiritual leader in the family and to others. Draw my father out of darkness into your marvelous light. Make the impossible possible for him and deal with him in miraculous ways all the days of his long and healthy life. Thank you for the salvation of my brothers and their mates and children and grandchildren. Radically save and set my brothers on fire with the gospel of Jesus Christ. Lift them high and mighty in the spirit realm and transform them from rags to riches. Make ways for them where there is none and open doors unto them that cannot be close. Bless them with righteousness, sanctification and purification. Deliver them from sin and death and give them eternal life. Cause my brothers to be leaders in the church and in their family. Loose their angels to bring them into their destiny with Christ. Cause your face to shine upon their face. Light a fire of love in their heart for you Lord. Place a burning desire in them to seek you out. Cause them to hunger and thirst after your righteousness. Establish them now in Jesus name. Remove every hindrance and every obstacle that stands in their way of salvation. Turn their stumbling blocks into stepping blocks and take them to great heights with you Lord. Clean and restore their hearts in Jesus name. Speak to them Lord in every sleeping and waking moments of their lives. Change their desires to your desires and give them peace and contentment in you Lord. Cause the spirit of reverence to be their abode and magnify yourself upon them. Lord, thank you for the salvation of my sisters and their children and grandchildren. Fill my sisters with the Holy Spirit and use them for your glory. Change them from the inside out and establish them as children of El-Eliyon, the Most High God. Baptize them with fire and give them the gifts of healing and miracles. Purge, cleanse and restore my sisters to their rightful place in your kingdom. Loose every bonds of Satan off them and cause them to walk into your marvelous and glorious anointing of signs and wonders. Anoint them as mighty warriors for your kingdom. Lord use them as weapons of your warfare that has been crafted in your fiery furnace. Surround them with your glory and anoint them to walk in the fullness of your power for their lives. Bring anointed men of God with integrity to be their husbands. Use their children to destroy Satan's kingdom of darkness. Bless these children with ministry and their own businesses. Draw my sisters out of deep waters and magnify yourself upon them. Bring them before great men and women and use their talents and gifts to make room for them. Lead them the way they should go and use their failures and defeats to be a blessing unto them. Restore to them every thing that the enemy has stolen. Make the darkness in their life light and their weakness strength. Crown them with glory and honor. Give them joy, peace and happiness. Raise them up to be leaders in the kingdom of God. Anoint them to do the impossible and cause greatness to flourish upon them. Cause a great spiritual awakening in their soul and bless them with wealth, riches and prosperity. Bless them in every good works and move quickly on their behalf. I decree and declare the spirit and anointing of Prophetess Deborah upon my sisters in Jesus name. Amen.

FINANCIAL PROSPERITY

It is written, beloved I wish that you would prosper and be in health as your soul prospers. Therefore, I am rich, walking in wealth, riches and prosperity. The Lord has blessed me and made my name great upon the earth. I have no lack for all of my needs are met in Christ Jesus. I have abundant supply of all that I need. I find handful of money left behind on purpose. I am reaping more than I am sowing. I reap where I have not sown. I have abundance to give out of. I am blessed to be a blessing to others. God will give me the treasures of darkness and hidden riches stored in secret places. I am blessed in the city and I am blessed in the country. God is causing men to give unto my bosom good measure press down shaken together and running over. My checking and savings accounts are in line with the word of God. I am overflowing with God's blessings. My hands are blessed to create wealth. I am industrious and faithful to my responsibilities and obligations. I am a world over comer with great financial testimony of how the Lord has blessed me to be a blessing. I am not a victim of poverty because I rebuke the spirit of poverty in Jesus name. I thread upon the spirit of poverty and break every generational curse that is associated with poverty in my family now. I plea the blood of Jesus Christ upon my finance and decrees the law of multiplication upon my money in giving and receiving according to the promises of Abraham. I am rich lacking nothing for Jesus lives in my finance and me. God has commanded his blessings upon me to overtake me. Everyday I awake I receive new financial miracles daily in Jesus name. God has clothes me in royalty, prosperity and notoriety. God has dressed me in wealth and riches for his namesake. My wealth has come now in Jesus name. I am blessed for sowing beside many waters. I shall become rich because God said it and Jesus died and took the curse of poverty for me so I could become rich in all things. God has caused me to dance on money. I have abundance and no lack is in my life. I have spiritual, financial, emotional, physical and natural prosperity, wealth and power upon the land. God has done great things to me. He has blessed me and caused me to prosper as my soul prospers. I have more than enough finance that never runs dry. God has caused men to give money unto me. I am debt free. God has restored my finances to build up the kingdom of God and to be a blessing to others. The gates of hell shall not prevail against my finances and hell shall not rob me of my finances in Jesus name. All my needs are met in Christ Jesus. I have no lack. I have more than enough for God has blessed me to be a blessing to others. Because I have delighted myself in the Lord, he has given me the desires of my heart. God has established me according to his promise to Abraham and me. God has restored me my entire life all the way back to Adam. God has restored everything unto me that was due me. What God has for me it is for me and it shall surely come to me for God's glory and the establishment of the kingdom of God upon the earth. I declare that the heathen bring their wealth, riches, money and valuables to me. God has caused men to give money unto me for the work of the gospel. I bless thousands of people with homes, cars, business, clothes, food and education with the wealth that God has bestowed upon me because I am a wise steward. I win souls with the finances God has given unto me and I give to the preaching of the Gospel. I help pastors and churches that are in financial need so that God can be glorified. The wealth that God has blessed me with is not mines to heap upon myself but God's to distribute as he has directed and instructed me. No weapons formed against me in my finance shall prosper because Jesus has given me wealth for poverty. Lord your word said prosperity belongs to me and I thank you for establishing prosperity in my life and in the life of my children and my children's children in Jesus name. I have obeyed the voice of the Lord. God has set me high above all the nations of the earth and commanded his blessings to come upon me and overtake me. Thus I am blessed and all my enemies flee before me because the Lord has established me before all the nations of the earth. I bring all my tithes and offerings unto the Lord for I am not a God robber and God has rebuke the devourer for my sake. I have proved God according to my faith and his word and he has opened the windows of heaven and poured me out blessings more than I have room enough to receive. Therefore, I am a delightsome sight upon the land and all the nations call me blessed in Jesus name I pray. God remember your covenant of prosperity to me and my family. I am a covenant tither and expects to receive all the benefits of tithing according to your words. Lord you promise to prosper me and bless the work of my hands and cause me to be a blessing to other.

PROSPERITY

The Lord is my shepherd; I shall not want. God prepared a table before me in the presence of mine enemies. God has anointed my head with oil and my cup runs over. Goodness and mercy follows me all the days of my life and I will stay in the house of God forever. God knows my works, and tribulation and poverty, but I am rich. My God shall supply all my needs according to his riches in glory. God has given me power to get wealth. Everything I do prosper. God has given me riches, wealth and honor. I shall spend my days in prosperity and my years in pleasure. Wealth and riches are in my home for God has brought me out into a wealthy place and I increased in riches. For wealth and riches shall always be in my house. Peace is within my walls and prosperity is in my palaces. Riches and honor are with me. My hand hath found as a nest the riches of the people. God will give me the treasures of darkness and hidden riches of secret places. I shall eat the riches of the gentiles. Blessed be the Lord; for I am rich. The wealth of the wicked belongs to me in Jesus name. I am debt free. I claim the Lord's release for all my bad debts. Therefore, I am out of debt. I decree and declare that I owe no man anything except to love them. God has given me an abundance of wealth for my poverty. I walk in prosperity and I am very prosperous. All my needs are met and all my desires are fulfilled in Jesus name. Heavenly Father, I thank you for prospering me in every area of my life and for establishing prosperity in my family. I thank you Lord for sending prosperity now into every barren area of my life in Jesus name. Mammon in the name of Jesus

Christ I command you to release my finances. For it is written that God owns all the silver and all the gold. Mammon in the name of Jesus I break your hold over my finances and I declare your defeat at the cross of Calvary where Jesus bore my poverty so I could be rich. Mammon in the name of Jesus I resist you and you must flee, for it is written resist the devil and he will flee. Mammon I raise my shield of faith against you in the name of Jesus. Mammon I resist you and overcome you with the blood of Jesus and the word of my testimony. God is my source. God is my provider. God is my shepherd and I shall not want for all my needs are met according to Jesus riches in glory. I have no lack in my life. I have abundance. I have sown finances and shall reap finance in abundance. I reap where I have not sown. God has caused men to give unto me good measure press down shaken together and running over. God has caused men to give finances and money unto me in the name of Jesus. God has open up the windows of heaven and is pouring out blessings more than I have room to receive. I am rich walking in health, wealth and prosperity. For every dollar I release, I command five hundred dollars in return in Jesus name. Money answers all things and I have plenty of money to answer everything in Jesus name. The wealth of the wicked belongs to the just. And the just shall live by faith. For it is written that God gives the heathen travail to heap up wealth and possession to give unto the righteous. Therefore, I command wealth to be given unto me in the name of Jesus for the establishment of the kingdom of God and the preaching of the gospel to all nations. I am rich because I am a born again believer. The rich rule over the poor and the borrower is servant to the lender. Therefore, I am ruling over the non-believers. I am the head and not the tail. I am going over and not under. I am on the top and not the bottom because I am Abraham's seed and an heir of salvation which entitles me to the promises of Abraham's covenant blessings. I am blessed and cannot be curse for who God bless no man can curse. I pay my tithes and give liberal offerings with great joy and thankfulness and I receive many fold blessings. I am prosperous and walking in prosperity. My family, friends and enemies call me blessed of the Lord God Almighty. Wealth and riches are in my house. I have peace in my finance I have the peace of God that surpasses all understanding in my finance. God gives supernatural and miraculous blessings in my finances. Mammon, I bind you with chains and shackles of iron and cover you with the blood of Jesus and command you to loose all my finances from the east, west, north and south right now in Jesus name. East I command you to loose my finance right now in Jesus name. West I command you to loose my finance right now in Jesus name. North I command you to loose my finance right now in Jesus name. South I command you to loose my finance right now in the name of Jesus. Money and currency I loose you in the name of Jesus to come into my possession right now for the establishment of the kingdom of God and for meeting all my needs. God I put you in remembrance of your unfailing words that cannot return to you void but must accomplish its works. You said I should prove you now and see if you will not open the windows of heaven and pour me out a blessing that I will not have enough room to contain it.

PROSPERTITY OF COUPLES

Lord, prosper the works of our hands and cause us to have great success in everything that we do. Lead us into successful opportunities all the days of our life. Cause us to flourish in rainy season and to have abundance in drought. Let us never borrow but always lending. Cause us to be blessed beyond measure and to be a blessing to others. Let the destroyer that rises against us be destroyed by the living God of gods. Spoil the spoiler who attempts to destroy our labor and our fruits. Our labor is not in vain because what we do for Christ will last forever. Lord, rise up against them that rise up against us. Bless them that are a blessing towards us. Curse them that attempt to curse us and turn the curse into a blessing for us; because, who God bless no man can curse. Grant us the abilities to pay all of our bills before the due dates and cancel all our debt and all our outstanding bills. Cause our checking, savings and investment to multiply like the little boy's 5 loaves and 3 fishes. Bless our tithe and offerings and give us miraculous breakthrough when we give sacrificially unto you. Let us give as we have proposed in our hearts to give, cheerfully in agreement with each other. Tell us when to give and when not to give. Teach us how to be good steward over what you have entrusted us with. Cause a little to multiply and produce an abundant supply of harvest. Bless all our seed and protect them from the devourer and the thief. Lord, give us seed to sow and give the increase. Cause us to see your prosperous ways in all areas of our life. Magnify yourself in us and let us be a testimony of your greatness for prospering your people. Let the heavens open up and pour out blessings and prosperity upon us. Cause us not to love money but rather to respect and appreciate money. Let us give freely to those in needs and to those causes that glorify you and do your will. Teach us how to be wise stewards over all that you have blessed us with in Jesus name. Amen.

DESIRES OF THE HEART FOR MATES

It is written, if I delight myself in the Lord, He will grant me the desires of my heart. I thank you Lord that my mate will come quickly and swiftly to my side and we will walk as one. I thank you that we will be joined in unity in the natural and spiritual realm. I pray that my mate's way will be straight before the Lord. I pray my mate will find joy and happiness in our marriage all the days of our lives. I pray my mate will never lack anything in our marriage. I pray all their emotional, physical, psychological and spiritual needs will be met in our marriage. I give thanks unto the Lord for providing me with the perfect mate. I pray that our marriage will be filled with lots of laughter, fun, excitement and contentment. I pray that we will never fight, argue or disagree to disagree. I pray that our marriage will be an example to many and that the Lord will bless us to be a blessing to other married couples worldwide. I pray that God will always be the nucleus of our marriage. I pray that my mate's sexual desires and fantasy will be fulfilled in our marriage. I pray that my mate will love and honor me and never forsake me. I pray my mate will love and enjoy all that I do in the home and at work. I pray my mate will be a good mate, parent, provider and leader and role model in our marriage. I pray my mate will meet all my needs to the fullest, my spiritual, emotional, physical, psychological, and sexual and any other needs I may have. I pray that our sexual relationship is impeccable, totally satisfying and beyond measure with great care, sensitivity and pleasure. I thank you Lord that our marriage was made in heaven and ordained before the foundation of the earth. We are a blessing to each other and produce children that are bless to be a blessing to others and us. We create wealth together and build upon the promises of God for our life. Let the vows we take become real to us: in sickness and in health, for better or for worse, until death do us part. Let us hold on to the confession of our faith and submit one to another without resistance. Together we are one and apart we are one in Jesus name. Amen.

SEEKING A HUSBAND

Behold the Lord will send me a husband for it is not good for me to be alone. The Lord will prepare the way before me and perfect the things that concern me. The husband I seek shall suddenly come to me. The Holy Spirit will bring him unto me wherever I am. Behold the Lord shall deliver a man of honor and statue unto me. The Lord has spoken my husband into my life. The Lord shall bring me a husband of my hearts desire and my husband shall make his way prosperous marrying me. For it is written, he who finds a wife finds a good thing and receives favor from God. Lord, I thank you that my husband finds me. Lord, I thank you for making me into a desirous and virtuous woman for my husband. Lord, I believe you have given me a husband for a covering and I declare I am my husband's glory. My husband is my head and I call him forth now to take his rightful place in my life. It is also written; let every woman have her own husband. I stand on your word as you watch over your words to perform them. For behold I am a fair woman for a man to look upon. Now Lord, according to your words do all that I desire and bring me a husband that will give you glory and cause my joy to be full. Amen.

CONFESSION OF FAITH

God has blessed me with wealth, riches and honor as he ought promised.

God has given me all power in heaven and in earth to do the greater works of Christ.

I am the head only. I am above only and I am a lender and not a borrower.

Wealth and riches are in my house and prosperity in my palace.

I have power to raise the dead, heal the sick and cast out demons and do the impossible.

God has made my name great in all the earth.

God has lengthened my cords and increased my boarders and enlarged my coast.

I have joy, happiness and the peace of God.

God is my provider, my shield, my defense and my strength.

I speak the oracles of God without discrimination.

Signs and wonders follows me because I believe.

No weapons formed against me shall prosper. The Lord will fight for me; for this battle in not mines it is the Lord.

PRAYING THE PSALMS

SELECTED SCRIPTURES FROM THE BOOKS OF PSALMS

NADINE A. ANDERSON

96

PAGE OF CONTENTS

Introduction 98

Book One 99

Book Two 105

Book Three 108

Book Four 110

Book Five 112

INTRODUCTION

Prayer is the answer to every question, every concern and every problem that faces mankind. Therefore, I offer this book to you as a gift and as a tool to achieve a closer walk and a more intimate relationship with God. Prayer has been my love and passion and this book is the fruit of my relationship with God.

I am always learning and growing, nevertheless, God is always speaking to me through his word, even when I am not listening. Nevertheless, I did not neglect to obey God when he told me to write and publish this book. This book may not be fancy or perfect but it will bring healing, salvation and deliverance to many and for this I am blessed.

I have personalized praying the psalms and made praying the psalms easy and understandable for both adults and children. The scriptures mentioned in this book are used as a reference guide to help the readers find the verses in the bible.

This book is copyright protected and should not be reproduce in part or whole without the author's consent.

Contact:

Nadine Anderson
144 East Dean Street
Freeport, NY 11520
(516) 557-6367
NAndersonBooks@aol.com

PRAYING THE PSALMS

BOOK ONE

Blessed is the man that walketh not in the counsel of the ungodly, nor standeth in the way of sinners, nor sitteth in the seat of the scornful. But his delight is in the law of the Lord; and in his law doth he meditate day and night. And he shall be like a tree planted by the rivers of water, that bringeth forth his fruit in his season; his leaf also shall not wither; and whatsoever he doeth shall prosper. (Ps. 1:1-3)

Father in the name of Jesus Christ your son give me the heathen for mine inheritance and the uttermost parts of the earth for my possession. Blessed are all they that put their trust in God. (Ps. 2:8, 12)

But thou O Lord, art a shield for me; my glory, and the lifter up of mine head. I will not be afraid of ten thousands of people that have set themselves against me round about. Salvation belongeth unto the Lord, thy blessings is upon thy people. (Ps. 3:3, 6, 8)

But let all those that put their trust in thee rejoice: let them ever shout for joy, because thou defendest them; let them also that love thy name be joyful in thee. For thou, wilt bless the righteous; with favor will thou compass him as with a shield. (Ps. 5:11-12)

Depart from me all ye workers of iniquity; for the Lord hath heard the voice of my weeping. (Ps. 6:8)

Oh let the wickedness of the wicked come to an end; but established the just. The wicked mischief shall return upon his own head, and his violent dealing shall come down upon his own crown. (Ps. 7:9, 16)

Out of the mouth of babes and suckling hast thou ordained strength because of thine enemies and the avenger. (Ps. 8:2)

The Lord has rebuked the heathen and destroyed the wicked. The wicked shall be turned into hell, and all the nations that forget God. (Ps. 9:5, 17)

Thank you Lord for arising and lifting up your hand for you have not forgotten me as I have humbled myself unto you. Break the arm of the wicked and evil man that stand against me; seek out their wickedness and destroy until there be no evil sent against us and our ministry. Lord, because you are the everlasting King the heathen perish out of this land. Lord, because you have heard my desire as I humble myself you have caused my ear to hear. (Ps. 10:12, 15-17)

Lord, thanks for saving me in my affliction and bring down the high lookers. The God of creation have light my candle and have enlightened my darkness. For by God, I have run through a troop, and leaped over a wall. God's way is perfect his word tried and true. He is a buckler to me because I trust him. (Ps. 17:27-30)

I thank you Lord that the words of my mouth and the meditation of my heart are acceptable in thy sight, O Lord, my strength and redeemer. (Ps. 19:14)

Thank you Lord for being my shepherd; I have no want or need of anything because you have provided all that I need even before my birth. In the presence of my enemies you prepared a banquet of blessings for me. You anointed my head with oil as a sign that I am covered with the blood of the lamb and the devil and his followers can't touch me to destroy me. My cup is filled and runneth over in the middle of my storms and adversities because with each affliction comes blessings of untold wealth. (Ps. 23:1, 5)

Lord, because I trust in you I will not be ashamed nor will my enemies triumph over me. Lord, because I wait on you, lead me into your truth and teach me your ways for you are the God of my salvation. Forget my sins and transgression because of thy grace and mercy remember only my goodness O Lord my God. Because I fear you Lord you have revealed to me your secrets and have shown me your new covenant which is your word written upon my heart that I will not sin against you. Lord, I look to you for everything because you are my only source; therefore, you have plucked my feet out of the net of destruction. Let the integrity of my words and the uprighteousness of my actions preserve me, for I wait on thee. Redeem me, O Lord out of all my troubles. (Ps. 25:2, 5, 7, 14-15, 21-22)

Judge me, O Lord, for I have walked in mine integrity: I have trusted also in the Lord; therefore I shall not slide. Test me O Lord and correct me, try my mind and my heart and establish me with dominion and power. (Ps. 26:1-2)

Lord, thank you for being my light and giving me directions in darkness. You are my salvation. Therefore, I no longer live in sin, because you O Lord are my strength. I fear no man or demon because you uphold me in your righteous right arm and fight all my battles for me. Lord, I desire to dwell in your presence all the days of my life and to behold your beauty. You asked me to seek your face daily and I did it and by this I know I will remain before you all the days of my life. Show me your pathway Lord so I will escape the tricks of mine enemies. Lord, I thank you for not delivering me over to the hands of mine enemies with their false witness and cruel hearts. I would have fainted had I not known about your mercy and your grace but because I believed in your words I saw your goodness in my life every second of every day. Oh Lord, I waited and I waited on you I was not always of good cheer or of a perfect heart but I remained in good coverage and you strengthened my heart. When I failed and thought all was lost, I became blinded by my emotions because I could not see your work in the background of my life and how you were perfecting the things that concerned me. I humbled myself and prayed and you opened my eyes to see that in serving you, God has exhalted me in high places. (Ps. 27:1, 4, 6, 8, 11-14)

Lord, I bless you with my whole heart for you have lifted me up and have not made my foes to rejoice over me. Lord, thank you for healing me when I cried out unto you. I shall not be moved in my prosperity. Mighty God, thank you for putting off my sackcloth and turning my mourning into dancing and empowering me with gladness. (Ps. 30:1-2, 6, 11)

Lord, I thank you for bowing down your ears unto me and delivering me speedily, you are my strong rock and my house of defense come and save me with your deliverance. I commit my spirit into your hands for you have redeemed me with your truth O Lord God Almighty. Let the lying lips be put to silence, which speak grievous things proudly and contemptuously against the righteous. (Ps. 31:2, 5, 18)

Let everything and every body fear the Lord and be in awe of him. Thank you Lord for speaking your promises for my life into being and establishing all that you have spoken unto me. Lord I know your eyes are always upon me because I fear you and hope in your mercy. You have delivered my soul from death and kept me alive in famine. (Ps. 33:8-9, 18-19)

I looked for you Lord and I found you. I prayed unto you and you heard me and delivered me from all my fears. The angels of the Lord surrounds me and delivers me. I keep my tongue from speaking evil and my lips from speaking guile. I departed from evil and I do good and seek peace in every situation. I thank you Lord for focusing on me and hearing my prayers because the prayers of the righteous availeth much are not in vain. When I was broken in spirit you surrounded me and saved me because of my broken heart and contrite spirit. Many are my afflictions, but Lord, you will deliver me from all my afflictions and destruction. (Ps.34:4, 7, 13, 15, 17-19)

Lord, your loving kindness is excellent; thus I put my trust under the shadow of your wings. I will be abundantly satisfied with the fatness of God's blessings and I will drink the rivers of my pleasure. I will not let the spirit of pride come against me nor permit the wicked to move me. The workers of iniquity that rises against me are fallen, cast down like Satan from heaven, rendered powerless over me and shall never rise to attempt to harm me all the days of my life. (Ps. 36:7-8, 11)

Lord, because I have delighted myself in thee I have the desires of my heart. I have trusted in the Lord and committed my ways unto him and he brings his promises for my life to pass. Lord, thank you for making me a good person and ordering my foot steps because I delight myself in your ways. I wait on you Lord, I keep your ways and you have exalted me to inherit the land; the wicked are cut off from before me and I see it with my own eyes.(Ps. 37:4-5, 23, 34)

When I was poor and needy, Lord, you thought about me when no one else would, you helped me and delivered me without tarrying. (Ps. 40:17)

I am blessed for considering the poor and the Lord delivers me in times of trouble. All them that hate me whisper together against me to devise my hurt. An evil disease, say they cleaveth fast unto them; and now they lieth down they shall not rise any more to do me harm. Yes even my very close friends whom I trusted with my secrets and confessions, eat my bread have lifted up their heels against me. But the Lord was merciful to me and raised me up that I may requite and rise above them. By this I know that the Lord strong and mighty favors me because my enemies did not triumph over me. (Ps. 41:1, 7-11)

PRAYING THE PSALMS

BOOK TWO

As the hart panteth after the water brooks, so panteth my soul after thee, O God; as deep calleth unto deep so does my soul calls unto God, and I am saturated with his power, anointing and glory. Why art thou cast down O my soul? And why art thou disquieted within me? I hope in God: for I shall yet praise him, for the Lord is the health of my countenance, and my God. (Ps. 42:1, 5, 7, 11)

My heart is dealing with a good matter. I speak of the things which touch the heart of God. My tongue is the pen of a ready writer. I am fairer than many. Grace is poured into my lips. Therefore, God has blessed me forever. The King of Glory greatly desires my beauty, for He is my Lord and I will worship him. The daughters of the world shall bring me gifts and all the rich people of the world shall bless me and give me favor. I am the king's daughter filled with his glory dressed in purple and gold. God has made my name great to be remembered in all generations. Therefore, I shall praise God forever. (Ps.45:1-2, 11-12, 17)

Thank you Lord for the river, the stream that makes glad the city of God, for out of my belly flows the river of a never ending fountain, the holy temple of the Most High God. God is in the midst of me, I shall not be moved: God shall help me right now. I am still because I know you are God, God will be exalted among the heathens; God will be exalted in the earth. (Ps. 46:4-5, 10)

God has subdue the people under me and the nations under my feet. (Ps.47:3)

My mouth shall speak of wisdom; and the meditation of my heart shall be of understanding. I will incline my ear to a parable: I will open my dark saying upon the harp. I will not be afraid when the glory of the Lord increases upon me. (Ps. 49:3-4, 16)

Behold I desire truth in my soul and in my spirit shall God reveal wisdom unto me. Create in me a clean heart, O God; and renew a right spirit within me. I sacrifice unto you Lord my broken spirit; because, Lord you will not despise a broken and contrite heart. (Ps.51:6, 10, 17)

When I cried unto thee my enemies are turned back for God is with me. (Ps. 56:9)

My soul followeth hard after God, his right hand holds me up. (Ps. 63:8)

I am blessed because God has chosen me and drawn me near to dwell in his presence. I will be satisfied with the goodness of the house of God and of his holy temple. God visits me and waters me and saturated me with his anointing. God provides my harvest in due season. God abundantly make soft with showers and caused my growth and my increase God crown this year with increase and much fatness that cause droppings in my pathways. My dry places and wilderness is covered with the blessings of God and I greatly rejoice with joy. My business is clothed with wealth and prosperity and the world has produced her harvest. I shout for joy and sing. (Ps. 65:4, 9-13)

God, you are terrible in your works through the power of your greatness, my enemies submit themselves unto me. When men rode over my head, I went through the fire and the water but God brought me out into a wealthy place. I will go into thy house with burnt offerings. I will pay thee my vows which my lips have uttered, and my mouth hath spoken, when I was in trouble. If I regard iniquity in my heart Lord you will not hear me. But verily God hath heard me; He has attended to the voice of my prayer. Blessed be God, which hath not turned away my prayers or his mercy from me. (Ps.66:3, 12-14, 18-20)

Lord, thank you for the plentiful rain you have sent me, because you have confirmed my inheritance when it was weary and hopeless. Blessed be the Lord, who daily loadeth me with benefits, the God of my salvation. Because of thy temple at Jerusalem the promise land, shall kings bring presents unto me. (Ps.68:9, 12, 19, 29)

Thank you Lord for delivering me out of the mire, and letting me not sink: thank you for delivering me from them that hate me, and out of the deep waters. Thank you Lord for not letting the water flood overflow me neither letting the deep swallow me up, and letting not the pit shut her mouth upon me. (Ps. 69:14-15)

Lord, I thank you for increasing my greatness and comforting me on every side. (Ps. 71:21)

PRAYING THE PSALMS

BOOK THREE

Thank you Lord that I have made you a vow and have paid my vow unto you. Now all them that surrounds me will bring presents unto me that ought to be feared. (Ps. 76:11)

God, when I remembered you, I was troubled in my spirit; I complained and my spirit was overwhelmed, because your sons and your daughters have forgotten your ways. I am so troubled when I look upon the body of Christ that I cannot speak. The people don't want to hear the truth; because they have sensitive ears that hears what they want and their ears have become stopped as the deaf adder that cannot be charmed. I have considered the days of old, the years of ancient times. I call to remembrance my song in the night: I commune with mine own heart: and my spirit made diligent search. (Ps. 76:3-6)

God, I will give ears to your laws and incline my ears to the words of your mouth. I will not forget your testimony and the mighty works you did for your people. I remembered how you divided the red sea, rained manner from heaven, brought streams out of rocks in the wilderness. You even satisfied the lust of your people and consumed them in your anger and wrath; because they did not believed you or trusted in your salvation. They tempted you in the wilderness and you destroyed them. Father, teach me not to turn back from you and go back into the world, for if I do I shall surely die and spend eternity in hell with Satan and the truth of your word wrapped up in my heart.

God, let me never forget who you are and how great you are. Let not the lust of my flesh or the lust of my eyes defile me or betray me to destruction, but cause me to prevail against temptations and rise to your glorious expectation in my testing. Prove me God, and try me and know what is in my heart and perfect me into your glorious image of perfection. (Ps 78:1, 7, 13, 15-20, 22, 24, 29, 31-32, 41)

Thank you for defending the poor and fatherless: and doing justice to the afflicted and needy. Thank you Lord for delivering the poor and needy and ridding them out of the hand of the enemy. (Ps. 82:3-4)

Thank you Lord, God for being my sun and shield: you have given me grace and glory: no good things have you withheld from me because I have walked upright before you. (Ps. 84:11)

Lord, thank you for giving me that which is good and my land shall yield her increase. (Ps. 85:12)

I will sing of the mercies of the Lord forever: with my mouth will I make known thy faithfulness to all generations. God, you are the glory of my strength: and in the favor of God my horn shall be exalted. And God will beat down my foes before my face and plague them that hate me. Lord, thank you for making me higher than kings of this earth. Lord, visit my transgression with the rod and my iniquities with stripes. Lord, I thank you for not breaking your covenant with me, nor altering the things that has gone out of your lips concerning me. (Ps. 89:1, 17, 23, 27, 32, 34)

PRAYING THE PSALMS

BOOK FOUR

The Lord has covered me with his feathers, and under his wings shall I trust: his truth shall be my shield and buckler. No evil shall befall me neither shall any plague come near my home. Lord, thank you for giving your angels charge over me, to keep me in all my ways. Lord, thank you for satisfying me with long life and showing me your salvation. (Ps. 91:4, 10-11, 16)

I am flourishing like the palm tree: and growing like the cedar of Lebanon. I am planted in the house of God and flourishing in the courts of my God. (Ps. 92:12-13)

I know that the Lord is God, he has made me and not I myself. I am his people and the sheep of his pasture. (Ps. 100:3)

God shall arise, and have mercy upon me: for the time to favor me, yes the set time is now. (Ps. 102:13)

Thank you Lord for satisfying my mouth with good things: so that my youth is renewed like the eagles. (Ps 103:5)

Thank you for making your angels' spirits and me a minister of flaming fire. (Ps. 104:4)

I thank you for giving me the land of Canaan, which is the lot of my inheritance. Thank you for increasing

me greatly: and make me stronger than my enemies.
(Ps 105:11, 24)

I see the good of thy chosen that I may rejoice in the
gladness of thy nation that I may glory with mine
inheritance. (Ps. 106:5)

PRAYING THE PSALMS

BOOK FIVE

Lord, I thank you for breaking the gates of brass, and cutting the bars of iron in sunder. Thank you for sending your word and healing me and delivering me from my destruction. (Ps. 107: 16, 20)

Thank you that wealth and riches shall be in my house forever. (Ps. 112:3)

Lord, I thank you for increasing me more and more. (Ps. 115:14)

Lord, I have hidden your words in my heart that I might not sin against you. I meditate in your precepts and delight myself in your statues. I will not forget the word of the Lord. I have chosen the way of truth, give me understanding, and quicken me in your ways. I trust in the word of God. It is good for me that I was afflicted; that I might learn your statutes. The law of God's mouth is better unto me than thousands of gold and silver. I receive your faithfulness as unto all generation, because the law of God is my delight; I did not perish. I thank you Lord for upholding me by your words that I may live and not be ashamed of my hope. (Ps. 119:11, 15-16, 25, 30, 34, 37, 42, 71, 92, 116)

I prosper because I love God. Peace is in my walls and prosperity in my palaces. (Ps. 122:6-7)

My soul waits for the Lord, more than they that watch for the morning. I say, more than they that watch for the morning. (Ps. 130:6)

The Lord will perfect everything that concerns me. (Ps. 138:8)

I will praise God, for I am fearfully and wonderfully made: marvelous are the works of God: and this my soul knows very well. Search me, O God, and know my heart: try me, and know my thoughts. (Ps. 139:14, 23)

I stretch forth my hands unto God: my soul thirst after God, as a thirsty land. God, cause me to know your ways, wherein I should walk; for I have lifted up my soul unto you. Lead me into the land of uprightness. Quicken me, O Lord for your name's sake. (Ps. 143:6, 89)

Our sons are plants grown up in their youths; our daughters are cornerstones, polished after the similitude of a palace. My store houses are full, and my businesses produce thousands and ten thousands in the nations. (Ps. 144:12-13)

The blind eyes are open and the bowed down are raised up. (Ps 145:8)

The high praises of God is in my mouth and a two edge sword in my hand, to execute vengeance upon the heathen, and punishments upon the people. (Ps. 149:6-7)

THE CHURCH PRAYER MANUAL

PRAYING FOR YOUR PASTOR & CHURCH

NADINE A. ANDERSON

114

CONTENTS

Introduction 116
History of Prayer and God's Response 119
Prayer for Pastor 122
Prayer for Your Church 126

INTRODUCTION

How Do I Pray? Always start with a sincere desire to communicate with God and repentance of any known or unknown sins in your life. It is always best to enter into prayer with thanksgiving, praise and worship, then the reading of the written word of God and then your needs and direction of the Holy Spirit. In closing, exit with thanksgiving and praise. However, use your best discretion on how to pray due to your own unique style and preference.

What Do I Pray For? You can pray for anything, anyone or whatever you need or whatever God puts in your heart. Be careful not to pray against another persons will by trying to control or manipulate them through your prayers. This is called witchcraft prayer. Pray the perfect will of God by praying scriptures and remember that we reap what we sow.

Why Do I Pray? To fellowship with God and to have your every needs met, while giving God permission to bring his will to past in the earth. God is not a violator. God gave man dominion on the earth; therefore, he needs our prayers to give him permission to bring his desires to past. Prayer is a two way conversation whereas God speaks back to you through his words or by the Holy Spirit.

When Do I Pray? You should pray everyday or like Daniel, who prayed three times a day or as often as possible. There are times when God will wake you up in the middle of the night to pray or may give you a deep desire to pray anytime or anywhere. Be obedient to the leading of the Holy Spirit and pray when God urges you to pray, for your prayers may very well determine a life and death situation for another person.

Where Do I Pray? You should pray in your secret place for private prayers for yourself and loved ones. It is best to find a place where you can be alone with God so you can open up yourself to him without reservations. You can also pray in public for others, things and places. However, don't limit God; feel free to pray anywhere and everywhere at all times for all men and all things that concerns you.

It is written that we should pray one for another that we may be healed. But when we stand praying, we should forgive, so that our prayers may be answered; because, the fervent prayers of the righteous avails much and are not in vain. Therefore, when we pray we must believe that we receive that which we asked for; because, it shall be given unto us according to our faith. Jesus said if you ask anything in my name I will do it. Therefore, ask and you shall receive, but doubt not in your heart nor be double minded. For so does a man thinks in his heart so is he. God is a good God, who gives us the desires of our heart. So fret not yourself for the Lord is your shepherd and you shall not want of any good thing. For whatsoever you asked God for, you will receive.

I highly recommend praying for 30 minutes minimum daily and 3 hours daily if you are a mature intercessor and watch God's commanded blessings overtake you.

I also recommend weekly fasting and praying. This is a time to withdraw from your regular routines and everyday hassles of life to lay before God in a broken and contrite state of body, soul and spirit. Then you will walk into miracles, signs & wonders and experience the power, the anointing and the boldness of Jesus Christ to preach the gospel with power and demonstrations of God's grace and mercy. You will also be the recipient of a compassionate love from a passionate and magnificent God

History of Prayer and God's Response

Abraham prayed and God saved Lot and his family.

Abraham prayed and God gave him a son in his old age when it was impossible.

Isaac prayed and God opened the womb of his barren wife and gave them twins.

Jacob prayed and God blessed him and made him rich and delivered him from the fear of his uncle Laban and his brother Esau.

Joseph prayed and God remembered him in prison and blessed him with favor and made him a ruler over an entire nation.

Moses prayed and God made him a great leader and a mighty prophet to a rebellious nation and people.

Joshua prayed and God delivered his enemies into his hands.

Samson prayed and God restored and strengthened him to destroy his enemies.

Hannah prayed and God blessed her with a son that judged a nation in the power and fear of God.

David prayed and God delivered him from his enemies.

Nehemiah prayed and God favored him to rebuild the walls of the city of Jerusalem.

Esther prayed and God saved an entire nation of people from death due to the hatred of one man.

Job prayed and God restored him greater in his latter end than his beginnings.

The prophets of old and new fasted and prayed and God answered all of their prayers.

The apostles prayed and God showed up and performed great signs, wonders and miracles in all of his glory.

This little sinner girl was on her way to hell and didn't care, but one day, God called my name and I prayed unto him and He answered my prayers with salvation and made me his adopted daughter. WOW!!! God does not fail to answer our prayers; we fail to believe that God will answer us when we pray. We don't want to wait 10, 20 or 30 years for his answers to our prayers so we give up on him and call him a liar. Throughout my brief christian walk, I have never found God to be a liar but I have found myself to be a liar, a doubter and a deceiver of God's infinite abilities to deliver me in times of need. I have wavered in doubts and unbelief. I became double minded and questioned God in my foolish state of ignorance. I have drawn back many times and nullified God's word in my life and prevented his promises from coming to pass in my life. I have found favor in God's eyes for I am not completely destroyed for lack of knowledge but the spirit of God teaches all truth and have open my eyes to see and my ears to ear. Therefore, I cleave to the knowledge of God for it is my life.

PRAYER FOR PASTOR (Your Pastor's Name)

Heavenly father, grant (Pastor's Name) wisdom, knowledge and understanding into all things. Open the eyes of his/her understanding and enlighten him/her to the mysteries of God. Give him/her a spirit of boldness, power and love. Crown him/her with a sound mind and the peace of God that surpasses all understanding. Illuminate his/her mind with the word of God and increase his/her faith, trust and hope in God daily.

(Pastor's Name) is strong in the power and might of God. He/She trusts in the Lord and leans not on his/her own understanding but in all his/her ways he/she acknowledges God and the Lord direct his/her path. He/She accomplishes the work of God, not by might nor by power but by the spirit of God that lives within him/her. He/She is a man/woman that fears the Lord and is established amongst the nations.

God has sent his word and healed (Pastor's Name), no sickness, no disease or no infirmity will survive in his/her body or come near his/her home, business or ministry for God has given his angels charge over (Pastor's Name) to keep him/her in all his/her ways. He/She is healed in his/her body, mind and spirit. He/She is made whole because he/she believes and by his/her faith and through the beatings of Jesus Christ, he/she is healed from the crown of his/her head to the sole of his/her feet.

(Pastor's Name) is blessed and prospering. God is speaking to people and moving upon the hearts of men to give finances unto him/her to build up the kingdom of God. Men are giving money unto him/her to preach the gospel to all nations. He/She has no lack for all of his/her needs are met. God is his/her source and he/she wants for nothing for God has given him/her the desires of his/her heart. The windows of heaven are open and God is pouring out continual prosperity upon (Pastor's Name). The work of his/her hands prospers and brings him/her great wealth and prosperity. God enlarged (Pastor's Name) boarders, lengthened (Pastor's Name) cords and has multiplied (Pastor's Name) businesses a thousand fold. God has blessed (Pastor's Name) with an abundance of houses, lands, transportations and finances and has enabled (Pastor's Name) to be a blessing to others. (Pastor's Name) walks in the divine favor of blessings in every area of his/her life. (Pastor's Name) is a rich man/woman and lacks nothing.

Mighty God, anoint (Pastor's Name) with resurrection power to raise the dead. Anoint (Pastor's Name) with the healing power to heal all who have need of healing. Anoint (Pastor's Name) with power to cast out demons and to speak in new tongues. Anoint (Pastor's Name) to walk in the supernatural realm of miracles, signs and wonders. Anoint (Pastor's Name) to preach with demonstration of signs and miracles following. Give (Pastor's Name) nations for the possessions and the unsaved for an inheritance. Anoint (Pastor's Name) with leadership authority and dominion to rule in the midst of the people.

Protect, provide and bless (Pastor's Name) husband/wife, children and extended family. Make them into a defended city and secure them on every side. Reinforce and secure the edge of protection around them. Cancel and destroy every plans of the enemy for them and expose and cause to fail every plot and snares of the enemy for (Pastor's Name) and his/her family. Every spirit of witchcraft sent against them is cut down and destroyed in Jesus Christ name. (Pastor's Name) and family are covered in the blood of Jesus Christ and clothed with righteousness and armed with the word of God to win every battle victoriously in Jesus Christ name. They are blessed and cannot be cursed in Jesus Christ name.

(Pastor's Name) is willing and obedient and will eat the good of the land. All things are possible to (Pastor's Name) because he/she believes the word of God and does not doubt in his/her heart the things that God has spoken to him/her.

(Pastor's Name) is blessed with integrity of heart, mind and spirit. Thus God, I beseech you to pour out the spirit and burden of intercession upon (Pastor's Name) and cause him/her to do exploit in the kingdom of God. Bless and multiply (Pastor's Name) a thousand fold with the gifts and fruits of the Holy Spirit. Bless and increase (Pastor's Name) to walk daily in the fruits and the gifts of the Holy Spirit in Jesus Christ name. Anoint (Pastor's Name) to prophesy with great accuracy and precision. Anoint and enable him/her to hear and interpret tongues of the spirit fluently. God, grant (Pastor's Name) the gift of discernment and cause him/her to have discernment of spirits in Jesus Christ name I pray.

PRAYER FOR YOUR CHURCH

Lord, we thank you that the vision for (your church name) will tarry no more but will come to pass now in Jesus name. We thank you that the vision is plain and we are running with the vision. We thank you Lord for giving us this city and all it's sinner for our inheritance.

We thank you Lord that we have a covenant of health and healing with you. We declare we are healed from the crown of our head to the sole of our feet. We declare no sickness, infirmity or disease can come upon us because of our covenant. Lord, thank you for sending your word to heal us. We thank you that when Jesus died on the cross we were healed and we declare we are healed and are walking in the prosperity of health.

Lord, thank you for marriages. What God has joined together let no man put asunder. We bind the spirit of division and separation now in Jesus' name and loose the spirit of love and unity. We called every marriage restored, refreshed and ignited with new found love and admiration for each other in the marriage. We thank you Lord for being the nucleus in marriages and perfecting the relationships. They have no need for spoil of each other and do not commit adultery. They flee from temptations and escape from sexual traps.

Lord, I thank you for the single people in (your church name). You are their mates and thy lack noting in you Lord. They honor you in their body and they are holy before you and are sanctified vessels. I thank you for bringing their mates to them in due season. They do not commit fornication and flee youthful lust.

Lord, I thank you for blessing us with our children. They are the fruits of our womb and they are blessed. They are trees of life planted by the rivers of many waters and they produce many fruits of the spirit in season and out of season. They posses the gates of the enemy and are the weapons of our warfare. Great are their peace and no weapon formed against them shall prosper. Our sons are plants grown up in their youth. Our daughters are corner stones polished after the similitude of a palace. Wealth and riches are in their house. Their footsteps are ordered by God. God is in control of their lives and they will live and not die to declare the glory of God.

Thank you Lord for giving parents the wisdom, knowledge and understanding to raise Godly children rooted and grounded in the word of God. Bless the parents to be a blessing to their children and give them the power to provide for their families.

Lord, I thank you for the elderly people in the church. They are mothers and fathers to the body of (your church name). Their youths are renewed daily. They shall run and not be weary; they shall walk and not faint. They shall mount up with wings like eagles to declare the glory of God. Their strength is in the Lord and they are renewed daily. They shall bring forth fruits in old age. They shall have a word in season and out of season.

The ushers would rather be a door keeper in the house of the Lord than to dwell in the tents of wickedness. They usher in change and usher the people to the throne of God. They are the guards of the palace of God. They keep the hand of the enemy at bay.

The musicians and praise team usher in the praise and opens the windows of heaven for God to pure down his blessings upon the people. They worship the Lord in spirit and in truth. They are God's sanctified worshippers. Lord, thank you for the opportunity to proclaim the gospel of Jesus Christ to the world, locally, nationally and internationally. Lord thank you for giving us power, dominion and authority in the airways and byways to preach the gospel to all men.

Lord, send us where you would have us to go daily in our outreach program for the kingdom of God to come upon the earth. Remove every obstacles and stumbling blocks from our pathways. Open great and effective doors before us that no man can close to preach the gospel with power, signs, miracles and wonders following and make the crocked paths straight, be with us and give us wisdom and stand behind us and give us strength.

Lord, create a spiritual explosion in the youth ministry. Draw youths from near and far into this church by your Holy Spirit. Lead the youths in this city to (your church name), to experience the work of God. Anoint our children to prophesy and do exploits in the midst of the people for your glory. Let the children and youths at (your church name) be a testimony to the world, of God's goodness and mercy. Show favor to the children and youth ministry and cause them to walk in the realm of the supernatural with Jesus Christ as their Lord and Savior.

Lord, thank you for joy, happiness and the peace of God that surpasses all understanding for this body of Christ. Let this house of God be established as a house overflowing with love, joy, happiness, prosperity and peace. Lord, we lift up the hands of the leaders of (your church name) and we support them in the work of the Lord. We declare our leaders will go forth in the power and might of the Lord, God, Almighty, who is able to do exceedingly, abundantly above all we could ask, think or even imagined.

Lord, thank you for the new members. Strengthen them to walk before you without stumbling and falling. Lord, catch them when they fall and place their feet on solid ground. Be their strength and direct all their ways. Establish them to walk holy and acceptable before you O Lord in holiness and righteousness. Sanctify their soul, their mind and their body and use them Lord, for your glory. Give them a thirst, a hunger and a great desire for your holy words. Lead them into your truth and deliver them from all their fears. Be their God and perfect everything that concerns them.

Lord, fill (your church name) with fire, let the glory of the Lord rain down on us. Give us the yoke destroying anointing of God; so, we can go forth in your power to complete our assignments. Let the rivers that flows from the throne of God, flows in (your church name). Turn this place into a pool of water and springs of water. Let all that is thirsty come and drink from the fountain of God in (your church name).

Lord, you are Lord of the harvest, bring in the harvest of souls and let our church overflow. Bring them in from the east, west, north and south. Bring them in from around the world. Bring rulers, kings and queens unto us to be ministered to. Bring in the rich, the poor, the sick, the dead, the lame and the outcast; bring them upon the wings of angels. Tarry not O God, move with great speed to bring your word to pass, mighty God. Open the gates and let the righteous nation enter into the kingdom of God. Lord, loose the heavenly host of angels to bring salvation upon the earth. We need your help Lord to bring in the harvest. Pour out your anointing upon us to be effective witnesses of the gospel of Jesus Christ and productive soul winners in the kingdom. Send laborers to work in the field and fill your storehouse with the harvest of Souls in Jesus name.

We bind Satan and all demonic spirits and activity now in Jesus' name from this body. We loose the word of God to dismantle every weapon of the enemy and to defeat the enemy upon enemy territory. Lift up the standards draw the sword of judgment and take vengeance O Lord.

Lord, thank you for timely order in this body. We acknowledge you as God and give you our best. We reverence and fear you Lord. Therefore, we desire to please you. We come to church on time ready to serve you without resistance or reservation. Because you have given us so much, we give you everything because we own nothing, not even ourselves

We thank you that we are a praying people and a praying church. We know when we pray we are conversing with you and we thank you for intimacy with us in prayer. We call unto you and you heard us and answered us quickly. You showed us great and mighty things we knew not of, your word declares the fervent prayers of the righteous availeth much and is not in vain. I thank you that we pray in unity on one accord, in one mind and we see the glory of God manifesting in our midst. Lord, we ask that you send skilled workers in our midst to help lift the hands of our pastors and to carry the vision into fruitfulness. Lord, pour down the El Shaddai blessings upon this body now in Jesus Christ name. Bring forth the gifts and the fruits of the spirit now in Jesus Christ name. We thank you that the gifts of the spirit, edifies the body. Thank you for providing for us and protecting us this year. Thank you that you have revealed yourself to us. Lord let your will be done in our life, in our city and around the world as it is in heaven. Amen.

CHILDREN'S PRAYER
SCRIPTURES FROM THE BIBLE

Nadine A. Anderson

CONTENTS

God's Commandments 134

Our Father 134

My Obedience to God & Man 134

God is my Provider 135

Healing & Restoration 135

God's Commandments for my Life 136

God's Purpose for my Life 137

I Am a Mighty Warrior for God 138

Prayer for Ministry 140

Covering, Protection and Deliverance 141

To Forgive your Enemies 144

Blanks for Notes 146
Blanks for Notes 147
Blanks for Notes 148
Blanks for Notes 149
Blanks for Notes 150

GOD'S COMMANDMENTS

I will love God.
I will tell the truth.
I will not steal.
I will not kill.
I will worship God.
I will not have sex until I am married
I will not be jealous of others.
I will love my enemies and friends.
I will not use God's name in vain.
I will rest on the 7th day.

OUR FATHER

My father who is in heaven, how great is your name, your kingdom come. Your will be done on earth as it is in heaven. Give me your word daily. And forgive me my trespasses as I forgive those who trespass against me. And lead me not into temptation, but deliver me from evil. Amen.

MY OBEDIENCE TO GOD & MAN

I am a disciple, taught of the Lord walking in obedience to God's will, with great peace and good behavior. I obey my parents, adults, and teachers because they have rule over me. The word of God is in my heart. I am prospering in all that I do and lack has no place in my life; because, God is faithful to all generation. The hearing of God's word brings understanding into my life. I understand God's word and live according to His word. I am righteous by the grace of God; therefore, God hears my prayers. I do excellent in school and I have favor with my teachers and my peers. Father, in the name of Jesus Christ, I thank you for my parents salvation and ask you to cause them to live a righteous life style. I prophesy that I will be mighty upon the earth. Therefore, I choose to walk upright before God with a pure heart. I am blessed and cannot be cursed. Wealth and riches are in my home. I am saved and filled with the Holy Spirit and the evidence of speaking in tongues. I am blessed because I keep God's commandments. Amen.

GOD IS MY PROVIDER

God is my Jehovah-Jireh, who provides for all my needs. I have no need or lack of anything in my home because I have more than enough. God leads me besides blessing of unknown depth. God gives me everlasting life and leads me in his salvation and glory. As I walk through life's disappointment, destruction and danger, I have no fear, for God is with me. God's word comforts me and my prayer strengthens me. God presents me with unlimited opportunities in the presence of my enemies. I forgive and love all my enemies. I have the fruit of Love, Patience, Obedience, Respect and Kindness. God will give me the desires of my heart and grant me my prayer request by faith. I will worship and serve God all the days of my life. Amen.

HEALING AND RESTORATION

Lord, forgive me my trespasses as I forgive others that trespass against me and lead me not into temptation but deliver me from evil for yours is the kingdom of heaven, the power and the glory. I am a child of righteousness and great shall be my peace. I am healed of all my diseases for the Lord God almighty is my healer. The joy of the Lord is my strength. The Lord is my restorer and will restore all unto me in Jesus name. I am the child of God and declare my victory over all my enemies. God, I give you glory and thank you, for restoring prayer back in schools. I am a light to this world and shall inherit the earth. Everlasting father, bless my land and guide me by your hands. Keep me from all demonic powers and cover me with your blood. Lord, let your will be done in my life, in my home, in my city, in my state, in my country and in the earth as it is in heaven. Amen.

<u>GOD'S COMMANDMENTS FOR MY LIFE</u>

I am to God a kingdom and a priest and a holy nation. Bring me on eagle's wings and bring me to you Lord. I obey the voice of God and keep his covenant therefore I am a peculiar treasure unto God above all people, because all the earth belongs to God. I serve only the Lord God Almighty. I will not serve any other god or gods. I will not make or worship any graven images. I will not pray to any icons or false god. The Lord God is a Jealous God that will curse my first, second, third and fourth generation with my sins and the sins of my father and fore-fathers if I don't repent. God will show me mercy if I love him and keep his commandment. I will not swear by the Lord's name in vain. I will speak life and not death with my tongue. I bless others with my words because every word that comes out of my mouth I am accountable for and my words shape my life and my future. I say what I want and I have what I say. What I do not want I do not say because I believe with my heart that I shall have whatsoever I say. I keep the Sabbath day holy. I work six days and rest on the seventh day. I honor my mother and my father and my days are long upon the earth. I will not kill anyone. I will not steal. I will not lie. I will not be jealous or envious of anyone or anything. I will not commit adultery or fornication. I will not have sex until I am married because it is the law of God. My body is a living temple of God. I keep my body holy and sanctified in the presence of God continually. Amen.

GOD'S PURPOSE FOR MY LIFE

Father God, I bless your holy name. I give you honor and glory. Lord God Almighty, forgive me all of my sins and unrighteousness and make me whole. Lord, use me to be a prophet unto my generation and to help bring about your will on earth. Lord, give me visions and revelations on how I can please you. Father God, if I stray or am disobedient, speak to me audible if necessary but please do what you must to get me back on track to complete my assignments. Lord, bless me with money, silver and gold because Lord, you said you will cause people to give unto me a good measure press down shaken together and running over. Lord, I want the heathen for my inheritance and their treasures stored in secret places. Lord, use me to do many signs and wonders that will cause people to turn unto you. Lord, fill me with the Holy Ghost and let me lay hands on the sick and declare their health. Lord, let your angels encamp around me day and night. Let no harm befalls me. Remove all obstacles from my path as I do your work. Lord, open the windows of heaven and pour me out blessings continually. Lord, open all the doors on earth so I can proceed to do your will. Lord, let kings and rulers of nations bow at my feet and ask your forgiveness. Lord, appoint me as a son of God and give me complete power and authority over our common enemy the devil. Lord, grant me wisdom, knowledge and understanding. Lord, help me to build a great nation for your return. Father, open my eyes to see your perfect plan for my life. Father, help me to hear clearly from you. Father, open my mouth to speak truth, life and the word of knowledge. Lord, order my footsteps in your pathway. Lord, let me posses the gates of the enemy and speak with the enemy at his gates. Lord, keep the devil under my feet and strip him of all power to harm me or my assignment. Lord, save all my families, my brothers, sisters, mother, father, grandparent's cousins, nieces and nephews, aunts and uncles. Lord, also save all of my friends and all of my enemies. Amen.

I AM A MIGHTY WARRIOR FOR GOD

I am saved by grace, righteous in the sight of God. I am taught of the Lord and great shall be my peace. No weapons formed against me can nor shall prosper. The Angel of the Lord shall keep me in all my ways and there shall no evil befall me. The Lord will save my family and me. God knew me before I was formed in the belly. God sanctified me before I came out the womb. God ordained me a prophet to the nation and I shall go to all whom God sends me and shall speak whatsoever God commands me to say. God touched my mouth and put his words in my mouth and said be not afraid of their face for I am with you and I will deliver you. I will not walk in the counsel of the ungodly, nor sit in the seat of the unrighteous nor stand it the ways of sinners. But my delight is in God and his laws. I am like a tree planted by the rivers of many waters that brings forth fruit in season and out of season. My leaf shall not wither and whatsoever I do shall prosper. Wealth and riches shall be in my house. I speak the word of God and do the will of God. My only purpose is to serve the true and living God that made heaven and earth. I am the heir to the throne of Grace and I am a child of God, a servant of God; a beloved of God and the Bride of Jesus Christ and the prophet of God who is blessed of the Lord a thousand fold. I am A MIGHTY WARRIOR for God, who prays to God without ceasing. I am obedient, honest, trustworthy, faithful and truthful. I am of God and greater is the Holy Spirit in me than Satan in the world. I have integrity and God continues to increase my family and me more and more. God removes all obstacles from my pathway. The hand of God is upon me. The favor of God is my covering and the light of God is my guide. I am created to serve God and not man. I am fearfully and wonderfully made in the image of God. I have faith in God and I trust in God. I believe the entire bible and believe I will work miracles like Jesus Christ in abundance. I believe I can do what God said I can do and I will say what God tells me to say. I will not fear men. I give God all the glory and remain humble before him all the days of my life. Amen.

PRAYER FOR MINISTRY

I grew and waxed strong in spirit, filled with wisdom and the grace of God is upon me. I increased in wisdom and stature and in favor with God and man. The spirit of the Lord is upon me. God has anointed me to preach the gospel to the poor. He has sent me to heal the broken hearted, to preach deliverance to the captives and, recovering of sight to the blind, He has sent me to set at liberty them that are bruised and to preach the acceptable year of the Lord. My faith has saved me. Whosoever receive me in the name of the Lord, receives Jesus Christ. God shall avenge me his own elect speedily when I cry unto him for help and deliverance from my enemies day and night. Lord, not my will be done but your will be done in my life. Father, into your hands I have committed my spirit. Lord, open my understanding that I will understand the scriptures. I shall see heaven opened up and the angels of the Lord ascending and descending upon me all the days of my life. I know the voice of God and will follow his voice but the voice of a stranger I will not follow and will flee from the voice of a stranger. I live in Christ and Christ lives in me. I produce much fruit in the spirit because God's word lives in my heart. Whatsoever, I ask of the father in Jesus name I will receive if I doubt not in my heart when I pray and ask. Before God formed me in the belly, God knew me and before I was born, God sanctified me and ordained me a prophet unto the nations. The Lord is my light and my salvation. The Lord is my strength. The Lord is my shepherd. I shall not want of any good thing. Discretion shall preserve me and understanding shall keep me. I shall find favor and good understanding in the sight of God and man. I trust in the Lord with all my heart. I will not depend on my own understanding but I will depend on the Lords. I fear the Lord and depart form evil. I honor the Lord with all my substance and he has blessed me with abundance. Blessings are upon my head. I will receive the desires of my heart. I am taught of the Lord and great is my peace. I shall be established in righteousness. I shall be far from oppression; for I shall not fear and from terror; for it shall not come near me. Whosoever shall gather together against me shall fall. No weapons that are formed against me shall prosper; and every tongue that shall rise against me in judgment I condemn now in Jesus' name. Amen.

COVERING, PROTECTION AND DELIVERANCE

In the name of Jesus Christ and by the power of Jesus blood, in the authority of Jesus word given to me as a child of God, I bind Satan. I command Satan to leave in Jesus' name. I seal this room, this house, this city, this state, this country and all the members of my family, relatives, friends and enemies and all possessions, in the blood of Jesus Christ. I bind and reject all spirits in the air, in the wind, in the fire, in the other world and in the elements. I bind all satanic forces of nature. I loose the Holy Spirit in Jesus' name to take over and occupy every space that Satan has been evicted from. I bind and reject all spirits of confusion, all spirits of doubt, all spirits of disruption, all spirits of division, all spirits of deafness and dumbness, all spirits of disobedience, all spirits of

141

games, all spirits of retaliation, all spirits of distractions. I bind and reject all spirits of infirmity, all spirits of sickness and disease. I bind and reject all spirits of evil and death. I bind and reject all spirits of deception and error. I bind and reject the spirit of lie and ignorance and fear. I bind and reject all spirits of pride and arrogance. I bind and reject every sin of the spirit and the flesh. I bind and reject all spirits of hypocrisy in Jesus' name. I bind and reject all spirits of distraction and command they leave quietly without delay. I bind and reject all perverted spirits. I bind and reject Satan from my life. I renounce Satan and all the forces of hell from my life. I declare that Satan has no power over my life. I love God and I serve the true and living God. I walk in God's perfect will for my life. I loose the forces of heaven and Godliness in my life. I loose the power of the Holy Spirit in my life. I loose Jesus Christ in my life. I loose God in my life. I loose joy, peace and happiness in my life. I loose health, healing and restoration in my life. I loose greatness and newness in my life. I loose miracles, signs and wonders in my life. I loose truth, holiness, righteousness, faith, the mind of Christ, hope, trust, humility, selflessness to Christ, submission to God's will and purpose for my life. I surrender all to Jesus. I surrender all to God. I surrender all to the Holy Spirit in my life. I declare God's will to be done in my life and not my will in Jesus' name. I loose the spirit of wisdom, knowledge and understanding, the spirit of power and might in my life in Jesus' name. I loose my mind on things above, on the kingdom of God, on things that are holy, pure, true, virtuous, honorable, just, kind, and good. I loose the eyes of my understanding to open up to see God's perfect plan for my life and his pathway for me to follow. I loose my hearing to hear only the voice of God my father, Jesus my brother and the Holy Spirit my comforter and teacher. In the name of Jesus Christ my Lord and Savior, I break and dissolve every curses, spells, hexes, evil wishes, evil desires and hereditary seals. I come against all satanic vows, powers, forces, pacts, satanic sacrifices and voodoo practices. I break and dissolve all links with psychics, clairvoyants, astrologers, mediums, occult seers, satanic cults, fortunetellers, séance, ouija board, tarot cards and occult games of all kinds. Come Holy Spirit of God and fill this room, this house, this city, this state, this country and every area of my life with your presence and your power from corner to corner, ceiling to flooring, top to bottom and all around. I ask God in the name of Jesus Christ to loose all my guardian angels to fight for my promises given unto me by God Almighty. This I ask in the name of my Lord and Savior Jesus Christ by the power of His blood, in the authority of God's written word given to me as a covenant child of promise from the Holy Bible. Lord Jesus, I ask today for an infilling of the Holy Spirit. Fill all the empty spaces within me with your peace, love, healing and joy. I ask for an increase and release of all the gifts and all the fruits and all the powers of the Holy Spirit. I thank you Lord for wisdom, word of knowledge, faith, healing, miracles, prophecy, discernment of spirits, tongues, interpretation of tongues, deliverance, inner healing, teaching service, gifts of encouragement, gifts of leadership, gifts of preaching, gifts of joy and laughter; so that I may use all the gifts cheerfully for the glory of God. In Jesus name I pray amen. Amen.

TO FORGIVE YOUR ENEMIES

Dearest God, heal my pains and my hurts which was caused by my enemies. Teach me how to love and forgive my enemies for the evil they have wished me and the destruction that they have caused to befallen me. Teach me your ways O Lord and remove every trace of anger, bitterness, malice, unforgiveness and hatred from my heart. Father put a guard upon my heart and teach me how to guard my heart with all diligence for out of it flows the issues of life. Your word declares that out of the abundance of my heart I will speak; let me not deal harshly or treacherously with those that have harmed me and help me to pray for them with love, mercy and kindness always blessing them and never cursing them especially if they are your anointed. Let me never forget what David said about King Saul when Saul was hunting David to kill him because of jealousy. "The Lord forbids that I should do this thing unto my master, the Lord's anointed, to stretch forth mine hand against him, seeing he is the anointed of the Lord." Let me know that you will avenge me because vengeance belongs to you. Lord, I thank you that everything works for the good of them that love you. I recognize this opportunity as a blessing, by removing iniquity from my heart. I thank you Lord that you have allowed the enemy to attack so you can purify me and perfect my praise unto you. I hate pain Lord but teach me to embrace the pain, which produces glory, and anoint me for the greater works. Give ear to my words O Lord and bring your words for my life to pass. Teach me how to wait on you without murmuring and doubting your abilities to deliver me in times of trouble. Cause me to rise above my enemies' let not my foot slip from your pathway to my destiny. Remove the obstacles setup by my enemies and teach me how to pray blessings upon their life instead of curses. See my pain and distress and reward me for my humility. Turn curses sent against me into triple fold blessings. Almighty God, bless and prosper my enemies in every good works. Save and deliver them from death and destruction. Cause them to see their errors and lead them into repentance. Lord, I forgive my enemies their sins and trespasses against me. So heal me now O Lord that I can testify of your goodness and mercy towards me. Show me your loving kindness and bless me with your unmitigated peace that passes all understanding, in Jesus' name. Amen.

Notes

Notes

Notes

Notes

Notes

ISBN 141202778-0

9 781412 027786